Columbia University

Contributions to Education

Teachers College Series

No. 854

AMS PRESS
NEW YORK

Education for
Economic Competence
in Grades I to VI

An Analysis of Courses of Study
Illustrated with Sample Materials

By RUTH WOOD GAVIAN, Ph.D.

TEACHERS COLLEGE, COLUMBIA UNIVERSITY
CONTRIBUTIONS TO EDUCATION, NO. 854

Published with the Approval of
Professor Harold F. Clark, Sponsor

BUREAU OF PUBLICATIONS
Teachers College · Columbia University
NEW YORK · 1942

Library of Congress Cataloging in Publication Data

Gavian, Ruth (Wood) 1903-
   Education for economic competence in grades I to VI.

   Reprint of the 1942 ed., issued in series: Teachers
College, Columbia University. Contributions to educa-
tion, no. 854.
   Originally presented as the author's thesis, Columbia.
   Bibliography: p.
   1. Economics--Study and teaching (Elementary)--United
States. I. Title. II. Series: Columbia University.
Teachers College. Contributions to education, no. 854.
LB1584.G35 1972   372.8'3   77-176800
ISBN 0-404-55854-2

Reprinted by Special Arrangement with Teachers
College Press, New York, New York

From the edition of 1942, New York
First AMS edition published in 1972
Manufactured in the United States

AMS PRESS, INC.
NEW YORK, N. Y.   10003

Acknowledgments

To MY sponsor, Professor Harold F. Clark, I am indebted for the inspiration received from his courses, "Education and Economic Welfare" and "The Teaching of Economics," and for his interest and encouragement while this investigation was under way.

At various stages in the work I benefited from suggestions made by Professors Ralph Spence, Erling M. Hunt, Benjamin R. Andrews, Ernest G. Osborne, Lois Mossman, Lester Dix, William B. Featherstone, Fannie W. Dunn, Roma Gans, and Miss Gertrude Belser, who were all most generous of their time and thought.

To Professor H. B. Bruner of Teachers College, and to Miss Helen H. Heyl, Chief of the Bureau of Curriculum Development in the Elementary Division of the New York State Education Department, I am grateful for placing at my disposal the courses and curriculum reports which furnished the raw materials of the investigation.

To Professor L. Thomas Hopkins of Teachers College and Professor Robert S. Lynd of the Faculty of Political Science of Columbia University, members of my examining committee, I am indebted for their penetrating criticism of the completed manuscript.

I am, of course, solely responsible for the views expressed and for any errors that may be discovered.

RUTH WOOD GAVIAN

Contents

CONTENTS

Education for
Economic Competence
in Grades I to VI

CHAPTER ONE

Introduction

THE NATURE OF THE DEMAND FOR ECONOMIC EDUCATION

IN RECENT years and especially since 1930, the demand has been growing that the public schools give more attention to the teaching of economics. Widespread unemployment and financial insecurity, the relief burden, the mounting public debt, and the failure of a large proportion of our people, because of insufficient or poorly utilized income, to obtain adequate diet, shelter, and medical care—these, and the efforts of the national government to deal with them, aroused a new interest in economics and a conviction that the ordinary citizen should know more about the subject. This conviction deepened as the nation confronted the tremendous economic readjustments required for its defense and anticipated those that would be necessary with the return of peace.

The demand for a wider diffusion of economic principles comes from divergent sources. One group fears the acceptance of new economic doctrines which are opposed to the existing system of private enterprise. Its members would have the schools defend the system and teach how private enterprises are run, in order that students might have more understanding of the problems of businessmen.

Another group emphasizes the importance of consumer education. This group has already won a wide following and has had considerable influence in the schools. As to the objectives of consumer education, there are several views. To some of its advocates the aim is merely to teach better "buymanship." Others would try to teach consumers not only how to get the most out of their money, but, by studying consumption standards and the management of personal resources, how to get the most out of life. Mrs. Dora Lewis, addressing a convention of the National Education Association in 1936, asserted:

1

Young people do much buying for themselves and their families. They should have help in recognizing that money has value only as it represents satisfactions in living that may be purchased with it and that the most important factor in intelligent spending is choosing for purchase things that contribute most to progress toward consciously selected goals. They need opportunities to consider comparative satisfactions that purchases may bring before making decisions about spending. [21:550] *

To a few the aim of consumer education may be no less than achieving by peaceful change an economy managed in the interests of consumers. There is no reason to think that this view represents the majority of consumer educators. Probably no organization is so influential in the consumer education field as the Institute for Consumer Education at Stephens College, Columbia, Missouri. In a 1940 conference announcement, the Institute endorsed by implication only such consumer education as is compatible with the present system of private enterprise:

We accept the following definition of consumer education: Consumer education is development in attaining the maximum individual and group satisfaction for time, effort, and money expended. We hold that consumer education, thus defined, will increase the efficiency of the system of private enterprise and will have a beneficial effect on public economic policy.

Others who favor more teaching of economics in the schools stress the importance of better occupational adjustment and distribution, which they believe can be brought about chiefly by (1) informing prospective workers as to the nature of the duties, the training required, the working conditions, and the lifetime earnings in the occupations in which they might be able to find employment, and (2) providing equal educational opportunities. When all young people choose their occupations in the light of adequate knowledge of all the occupations which they might enter, and none are excluded from any occupation because of inability to pay for the necessary training, real wages, it is argued, will tend to be adjusted until equal ability and effort are equally rewarded in every occupation. Moreover, the total output of goods and services will thereby be greatly increased, since millions of workers

---

* The numbers in brackets throughout the text refer to corresponding numbers in the Bibliography. The number preceding the colon indicates the number of the reference in the Bibliography; the number following the colon indicates the page cited in the reference.

will have shifted from occupations in which they can produce little to occupations in which they can produce more. Professor Harold F. Clark has developed this argument in his book, *Economic Theory and Correct Occupational Distribution.* [6]

Another group advocating that the schools give more attention to the teaching of economics believes that this is the only way to insure orderly progress in improving economic conditions which, if left uncorrected, may cause the downfall of democracy. Harry Sherman writes in *The Promises Men Live By:*

It must be apparent, indeed, to any person of reflection, that the universal ignorance which prevails about how society functions is the first and perhaps the most impervious of all the obstacles which stand in the way of orderly human progress.

From the long-range point of view, the program which this state of affairs demands almost seems to map itself out. It is a program of the widest possible economic education. . . . The next broad line of advance the human race will make—indeed, must make—will be in the direction of its own organization, that is, in self-understanding. And, manifestly, economics is the principal tool of knowledge by which that eventuality may be attained. But it must—this is equally clear—be a knowledge that is very widely diffused. [33:xx–i]

That the lack of such widely diffused knowledge is a danger to democracy is asserted by Newlon in the *First Yearbook* of the John Dewey Society:

The plain fact is that democracy is seriously threatened because it has as yet been unable to find a way of most effectively utilizing, through intelligent planning and control, the technological and material resources of the country for the benefit of all; instead it leaves these resources to the exploitation of a privileged group. The crucial facts relating to the development of economic policy in the United States at this time are, on the one hand, the conflict of interest groups, and, on the other, the relative ignorance of the great masses of the people with reference to the actual conditions and interests at stake. It has been demonstrated over and over again that when the American people know the facts with reference to important national problems, and are effectively organized, they will make and carry out decisions that are in the interest of the people as a whole. [28:293–4]

It is vitally important that the schools prepare future citizens to make wise decisions on the grave economic and political issues of our time—

such is the theme of the final report of the Commission on the Social Studies of the American Historical Association:

Within the limits of the broad trend toward social integration, the possible forms of economic and political life are many and varied, involving wide differences in modes of distributing wealth, income, and cultural opportunity, embracing various conceptions of the state and of the rights, duties, and privileges of the ordinary citizen, and representing the most diverse ideals concerning the relations of the sexes, classes, religions, nations, and races. From this vast range of possibilities the American people will be called upon to make more or less deliberate choices in the proximate future. [1:20]

In another passage of the same document the Commission deals more specifically with the need of education for economic democracy:

Recognizing the necessity of living in an integrated economy and aware that such economy may be made to serve either some privileged minority or the entire population, the Commission deliberately presents to education, and affirms the desirability of, an economy managed in the interests of the masses, as distinguished from any class or bureaucracy. [1:90]

In summary it should be said that those who favor more teaching of economics seek one or more of the following outcomes: (1) a favorable attitude toward the private enterprise system; (2) more intelligent use of income by consumers; (3) better occupational adjustment and distribution; and (4) a clearer understanding of present-day economic issues.

The demand for education directed toward these outcomes is reflected in recent reports of the Educational Policies Commission. In *The Purposes of Education in American Life* the Commission declares that the schools should promote personal economic efficiency and economic literacy in citizenship. Below is the Commission's outline of what is involved in economic efficiency:

OBJECTIVES OF ECONOMIC EFFICIENCY

1. *Work*. The educated producer knows the satisfaction of good workmanship.
2. *Occupational Information*. The educated producer has *selected* his occupation.

3. *Occupational Efficiency.* The educated producer succeeds in his chosen vocation.
4. *Occupational Adjustment.* The educated producer maintains and improves his efficiency.
5. *Occupational Appreciation.* The educated producer appreciates the social value of his work.
6. *Personal Economics.* The educated consumer plans the economics of his own life.
7. *Consumer Judgment.* The educated consumer develops standards for guiding his expenditures.
8. *Efficiency in Buying.* The educated consumer is an informed and skillful buyer.
9. *Consumer Protection.* The educated consumer takes appropriate measures to safeguard his interests. [10:90]

In another section of the same report the Educational Policies Commission discusses what is necessary for economic literacy as a citizen:

The citizen who is economically literate is acquainted with certain broad economic issues, conditions, and procedures. He has become familiar through frequent usage with currently important economic concepts, with the ideas of supply and demand, investment and profit, capital and labor, scarcity and abundance, monopoly, the market, wages, and prices. He is informed concerning the principal economic developments under public auspices, such as the Tennessee Valley power projects and the Social Security laws. He sees these trends and conditions in the light of their historic antecedents. He knows certain facts which are crucial to the economic life of the country—its basic physical and human resources, its potential and actual productivity, the distribution of incomes and wealth, and the degrees of concentration or dispersal of ownership and management. Only as a growing degree of competence and interest in these matters is diffused among the people can democracy function in the teeth of technological change. [10:117-8]

Elsewhere the Commission makes the following statement with regard to economic intelligence:

The rank and file of citizens must achieve that degree of economic intelligence permitting them to understand the meaning of the new forms which capital now takes, and to exercise the controls which will increase the assets and decrease the liabilities which it will bring to mankind. [9:35]

It is clear from these citations that influential organizations of educators are taking part in the movement to obtain more teaching of economics in the schools. However, it can hardly be said that teachers generally have shown great interest in the movement. One reason for this may be the belief that economics is concerned entirely with material well-being. Teachers are inclined to disclaim material values and to consider it a duty to teach children that happiness does not depend upon possessions. Can they be expected to interest themselves in a subject thought to deal only with values that can be measured in money?

Economics, it is true, is the science that deals with the production, distribution, and consumption of wealth. But wealth includes all those goods and services to obtain which men have to put forth effort—not only bread but birthday cakes, not only shelter but paintings and rose-bushes, not only life insurance but medical care and music lessons. The ultimate purposes of economic knowledge are: (1) that the production of wealth may be increased; (2) that wealth may be distributed more advantageously for the total welfare; and (3) that wealth may be consumed in such manner that it will best satisfy the greatest range of human wants. Taken together, these purposes are not materialistic but humanitarian.

The basic reason why the Commission [on the Social Studies] emphasizes problems incident to the transition in economy is not because life is conceived in gross material terms, but because the establishment of a higher and finer standard of living may be expected to free people from absorption in material things and enable them to devote greater attention to ideals of spiritual, scientific, and cultural development. [1:22]

NAMING AND DEFINING THE MOVEMENT

The movement to increase the teaching of economics has been somewhat hampered by the lack of a convenient and suitable title. Some of the names which have been used, such as "thrift education," "consumer education," "business education," "conservation education," and "household economics," are not sufficiently inclusive. Other more inclusive titles, such as "economic education" and "education for economic literacy," seem to emphasize the teaching of economic theory and terminology as if these were an end in themselves.

The teaching of economic theory and terminology as ends does not appeal to the growing body of educators who believe that only that knowledge which leads to a change in behavior can educate. Still less does it appeal to the ordinary citizen, for popular thought holds that economics is excessively abstract and that economists rarely agree either on theories or on their applications. Furthermore, there is a feeling that economic theories are used chiefly to justify the prevailing economic setup and to oppose economic reform. This distrust of economics is seen in the statement that "economics is the rationalization of the existing business structure."

Inasmuch as many of those favoring more teaching of economics hope that it will lead to changed behavior, in the area of either consumption or occupational choice or both, while others hope that it will lead to peaceful economic reforms, a title should be found that avoids the connotation of "economic education" or "education for economic literacy" and directs attention to the aim of sound action in the economic sphere. The title here proposed is "education for economic competence."

WHAT ECONOMIC COMPETENCE INVOLVES

Before considering the question of what is being done or may be done to educate for economic competence, it is necessary to decide what economic competence involves.

Economic competence is not precisely the same for a person whose income is derived from property ownership and for one whose income is derived from running a business; for a person whose income is derived from operating a farm and for one whose income is derived from a wage; for a person whose annual income is five thousand dollars or more and for one whose annual income is five hundred dollars or less. Nor is economic competence the same for the citizen living under a dictatorship and for one living in a democracy.

We are here concerned with deciding what is involved in economic competence for an American citizen in the ordinary walks of life. He may be a farmer or a small businessman, but probably he is a wage earner. His wife will do all the housework and at times will seek to increase the family's cash income by working outside the home. They will belong to that great group of Americans having little property, little or no savings, and obliged to manage their earnings very carefully in order to obtain the actual necessities of life. We know this because in 1935–36 —a year representative of average conditions—65 per cent of American families had an annual income of less than $1,500 [25:6]. The skills and understandings necessary if the ordinary American citizens are to be economically competent follow from the conditions under which they live. These skills and understandings may be considered under three headings: (1) competence as a producer; (2) competence as a consumer; (3) competence in economic citizenship. The following list is suggested as a reasonable minimum, both for men and for women.

Economic Competence as a Producer Involves:

1. Appreciation of good workmanship and the desire to earn one's living in a manner that adds to the total real income of society.

2. The ability to evaluate different occupations, including possible methods of self-employment, with respect to working conditions, earnings, steadiness of employment, emotional satisfactions, and social utility.

3. Adequate preparation for the occupation selected. Knowledge of the best procedures for seeking employment in that field.

Economic Competence as a Consumer Involves:

4. The ability to select consumer goods—food, clothing, textiles, shelter, home furnishings and equipment, toys, recreational equipment, supplies for the home medicine cabinet, household preparations, and supplies needed for the repair and upkeep of a home.[1]

5. An understanding of how to care for and use to the best advantage all the items covered in (4). Specifically this requires knowledge of:[2]

  a. The principles of cooking and meal planning.

  b. The best ways to care for food in the home.

  c. In rural and suburban areas, ways to preserve surplus foodstuffs.

[1, 2] While women do the bulk of the buying for the family and are chiefly responsible for the meal planning, the care of clothing, and the physical upkeep of the home, they are influenced at every step by the wishes of the men of the household. It is therefore desirable that men as well as women understand the principles which underlie the selection, care, and use of consumer goods.

d. The care and repair of clothing, including the altering and making over of garments.

e. The use of textiles in furnishing and decorating the home.

f. The care and repair of a house with its furnishings and equipment.

g. The care and repair of toys and recreational equipment.

6. The ability to select medical and other health services appropriate to one's needs and income. This is likely to require knowledge of services available at less than their full cost.

7. The ability to select recreations appropriate to one's needs and income and to evaluate their contribution to personal and family welfare.

8. Knowledge of common business and banking forms and their use—bills, receipts, checks, bankbooks, contracts for installment buying, leases, notes, deeds, and the like.

9. Knowledge of the cost and suitability of the various types of consumer credit and the various types of life insurance, and the safety of and return from ordinary methods of saving and investing, especially those available to persons of small means.

10. Knowledge of the cost and suitability for various purposes of the usual methods of communication, shipping, and travel.

11. The ability to manage one's income so as to obtain from it the maximum satisfactions. This involves the habit of weighing comparative values and costs; the ability to evaluate the claims made by advertising and salespeople; the ability to apportion the available income among the several needs of one's self and one's dependents, and to determine how much, if any, should be used for advancement, charity, insurance, and savings.

12. An understanding of the cost of living and an appreciation of the economic burdens involved in maintaining a family.

Economic Competence as a Citizen Involves:

13. The abhorrence of waste, whether it be of one's own resources, those of others, or those that are socially owned; in particular, an abhorrence of the unnecessary waste of any natural or human resource.

14. Acquaintance with the methods and purposes of organizations, such as labor unions, cooperatives, credit unions, consumer associations,

Farm Bureaus, and people's lobbies, through which persons in the ordinary walks of life may seek the economic betterment of their group or of society.

15. Economic literacy in civic affairs. This includes such items as:

a. The ability to participate intelligently in determining how tax money shall be raised and apportioned.

b. Understanding that government expenditures (except for war and for corrupt purposes) do not diminish the national income.

c. Appreciation of the relationship of adequate income to health and efficiency; understanding that social and government expenditures to raise all families to the health and efficiency level can be justified on economic as well on humanitarian grounds.

d. The knowledge that increased productivity, and not merely a redistribution of the current national income, is necessary for improving the scale of living of the masses of people.

e. Realization that one of the central problems of our time is to regulate production and distribution in the interests of all the people, while preserving and freeing individual initiative.

16. Appreciation of the possibilities for good and for evil inherent in machine production. This includes such understandings as the following:

a. Mass production operated solely for personal gain has both good and evil consequences. Among the evil consequences is the concentration of income and power in the hands of a small class.

b. Mass production when operated in the interests of society as a whole has tremendous possibilities for human welfare.

c. Our economy cannot operate successfully unless the earnings of the masses of people are adequate to make the products of industry available to all.

d. The United States has the natural resources, the labor, the capital, and the technical knowledge necessary for abolishing poverty and the fear of poverty.

17. Recognition of the main lines of economic change and hospitality to needed change.

The foregoing list includes only the skills, knowledge, and understandings thought to be essential to the economic competence of the average American. A good case could doubtless be made for the inclusion of other items.

Study of the list suggests (1) that education for economic competence must extend over a long period of years; (2) that it must give abundant practice in weighing alternatives and making choices; (3) that it should be closely related to the real economic problems of the students and the community. It is apparent that economic competence is not likely to result from exposure, however prolonged, to an academic type of schooling.

PLACE OF EDUCATION FOR ECONOMIC COMPETENCE

Whether education for economic competence should begin earlier than the junior high school period is questioned by many. Four arguments against beginning it earlier are commonly advanced: (1) Such education would expose children to adult problems with which they cannot cope and about which they are better left in ignorance. (2) Economics is unrelated to the experiences of children. (3) The necessary skills, knowledge, and understandings cannot be developed in the elementary grades and the attempt to do so will result in mere verbalisms. (4) Children of elementary school age do not, of their own accord, manifest much interest in the economic phases of life.

The first objection, that children should not be exposed to adult problems, is answered by Newlon in the *First Yearbook* of the John Dewey Society:

The work of the school should be adapted to the maturity of the learner. This does not mean, however, that young children are to be shielded from consideration of critical social problems that come within their own experience. The question is as to the extent to which such problems can be profitably explored by immature children rather than of the kinds of problems that should be considered. It is now almost universally agreed that the work of the primary grades should be concerned with the vital problems of everyday living of the children. This of necessity involves in one form or another the consideration, on the children's level to be sure, of many of the most critical social and economic problems of our times, even such problems as those of housing, diet, and of unemployment. [27:274]

Hockett makes a still stronger statement in response to those who would shield young children from knowledge of adult problems:

Elementary children are not merely preparing to be members of society; they *are* members. . . . Children are consumers of food, clothing, housing, water, public utilities, and a thousand other commodities and services. Children suffer bitterly from low standards of living, unemployment in the family, industrial strife, and insecurity. They are vitally affected by the success or failure of the community to safeguard the life and health of its people and to provide recreational and cultural facilities. . . . They are affected by omnipresent propaganda, skillfully designed by interested groups to form certain definite habits, emotions, and prejudices. No, children cannot be isolated or insulated from the life of the times. The supreme function of the school is to enlighten their developing experiences, so that they become better informed, more appreciative, and more critical of the many activities of social life. [17:140]

The second objection to beginning education for economic competence below the secondary school level is the claim that it is unrelated to the experiences of children. Perhaps this is true for children of families in the upper income brackets, especially if they live in boarding schools. It is not true for the great majority of children.

Most children are born and brought up in rural areas. They live on or near farms, where they observe a variety of primary production and marketing activities. They know personally the village storekeeper and the proprietors of other local enterprises. They hear their elders complain about taxes and the interest on the mortgage and the low prices of farm products. They are continually told that there isn't enough money to buy the clothes and playthings they ask for. At an early age they begin to do household and farm chores, and to seek opportunities to earn money. As soon as they reach ten years of age they may enroll in 4-H clubs to carry on small-scale farm enterprises, such as raising a hog or a flock of chickens and keeping a record of expenses and returns. And before they reach teen-age many have helped in activities to raise money for their Sunday school or church.

The average city child has less opportunity than the rural boy or girl to observe at close hand and participate in simple productive activities. He may have little notion of the way in which the family income is earned. But by the time he reaches six or seven he has begun to do errands at near-by stores, and he already knows that to lose a coin is a serious matter. He discovers early that his parents can buy only a few of the things he wants. He hears them talk over the family expenses and knows that these are a constant source of worry, if not of friction. Canvassers come to the door. So do insurance agents and bill collectors. Stores in the neighborhood fail and others take their places; he observes the "grand opening" and the bankruptcy sales. He learns after a while that the fathers of some of his playmates are unemployed or on work relief. He sees pickets pacing the sidewalk and reads their placards calling for higher wages and asking the public to boycott the employer. Surrounded by diverse and ever-changing economic activity, the city child has a wealth of direct and vicarious economic experience.

The third objection to beginning education for economic competence below the secondary school level is the claim that the necessary skills, knowledge, and understandings cannot be developed in the elementary grades.

It is obvious that few of the listed essentials for economic competence can be completely learned in the elementary school period. Yet, if left wholly to the secondary school period, some may not be learned at all and others may be learned imperfectly. The development of such mind-sets as appreciation of good workmanship, abhorrence of waste, the habit of weighing comparative values and costs, the habit of caution in responding to advertising, and the habit of evaluating occupations as to their social utility should begin as early as possible; it cannot safely be left until adolescence.

Of the wide range of information needed for economic competence, much is so simple and so clearly related to the child's everyday experiences that it can readily be introduced in the elementary grades, and is doubtless more interesting and appropriate there than on a higher level.

The real argument is whether the teaching of the understandings necessary for economic competence as a citizen should begin in the elementary school. The effort to teach them there, some believe, will result in the memorizing of verbal formulas which are without meaning to the child. This would seem to depend on the manner in which they are taught. No modern educator would advocate that generalizations be taught apart from experiences. But should the teacher refrain from developing the generalizations that help illuminate the experiences for fear that the child will not grasp them fully? To do so is contrary to what we know of the learning process. Economic principles, like other generalizations, must be taught over and over in situations to which the principle applies. The principle acquires meaning for the learner gradually, never all at once.

T. L. Kelley and A. C. Krey write as follows concerning learning in the social sciences:

> Learning in the social sciences is a constantly cumulative process which is only well begun by the time the pupil reaches the end of the public school system. Even the most simple of its ideas cannot be firmly grasped as a result of one incident or one statement of principle. Few of them are mastered even to the extent of a good working knowledge in any one grade. But their learning is begun as early as life itself and may be greatly accelerated by wisely directed instruction during the school years. [20:48] . . . Precision in the grasp of a fundamental fact requires a number of considered illustrations of its occurrence, preferably at intervals. Under the most favorable conditions, several illustrations are required, and usually many more are needed, to give the pupil an understanding of any term as it is commonly used. [20:116]

A. J. Stoddard, in an article on providing an adequate economic education, stresses the importance of beginning in the elementary grades:

> Economic education, like health education, civic education, esthetic and moral education, and proper training in one's language, is not a matter of a semester or a year but must run through a considerable proportion of the elementary and secondary curriculum. Separate courses in economics need not be taught in each of the several grades, but there is need for economic education in some form beginning with the kindergarten. . . . It is feasible because modern education, particularly in the elementary school, has set up an activity program and has so related this program to life experiences that it is a proper medium for a continuous program of economic as well as other education. [34:27]

The fourth argument against beginning education for economic competence before the high school period maintains that children do not, of their own accord, talk very much about economic matters. There is some evidence to support this claim. In an extensive study of the social and economic interests of children expressed by them in free discussion periods, the New York State Association of Elementary School Principals found that children in free discussion periods in the classroom do not seem much concerned with the economic phases of life and that they pay little attention to the economic problems of the nation and the world or to the economic aspects of current events; furthermore they do not talk about problems affecting their own lives. Of 14,235 comments and questions by 9,423 children in the first six grades, only 284 items were considered to show economic consciousness. [29]

That children do not publicly discuss personal economic problems is to be expected. Neither do adults. That children do not spontaneously discuss the economic phases of current events may mean only that they do not hear these subjects discussed by parents and teachers. In the absence of any stimulation from adults, they cannot be expected to talk about relationships not immediately obvious.

Elementary teachers who are themselves interested in economics do not find that children are apathetic in this area. On the contrary, children's keen sense of reality, as yet unobscured by the acceptance of the traditional, and their desire to understand human affairs, make it easy to awaken their interest in economic relationships. Newlon writes in the *First Yearbook* of the John Dewey Society:

Many aspects of social, economic, and ethical problems interest young children, as every kindergarten and primary teacher knows. [27:264]

This is confirmed by Bruner, writing in the *Teachers College Record* in 1938:

As numerous teachers will testify, it is becoming increasingly evident that we have not begun to plumb the possibilities in elementary education of assisting children on the proper age and grade level to understand and to participate with happy enthusiasm in simple but basic aspects of many social and economic issues. [3:274]

The arguments against introducing education for economic competence in the elementary grades do not appear very substantial ones. And there are at least three strong arguments in its favor: (1) The economic activities observed or shared by the modern child are fragmentary and require interpretation. (2) The life-centered curriculum is necessarily concerned with economics. (3) The child's economic education is going on all the time, and unless intelligently directed it will not be suited to existing and emerging conditions.

The first argument arises from the complex nature of our modern economy. Children share in and observe a great deal of economic activity, but unlike the children of a hundred years ago, they do not witness the whole economic process from the production of the raw material to its manufacture and ultimate consumption. Many intermediate steps have been added, some visible to only a few individuals. The modern child cannot master the patterns of economic life in childhood, as did the child of long ago. If he is to discern the patterns, he must have the help of adults acquainted with economics. Here, as in other areas of experience, the teacher's role is to assist the child to observe more closely and to interpret and become critical of what he sees.

According to the second argument, the life-centered curriculum is necessarily concerned with economics. Most of the energies of civilized men and women are devoted to economic activities—to earning and spending an income and to maintaining a home. No curriculum that is related to life can ignore earning and spending, producing and consuming. The social studies, in particular, constantly deal with events and relationships in which there is an economic element.

The child's economic education, runs the third argument, is going on all the time, whether directed or not. Attitudes are being built and understandings (correct or erroneous) of the nature of our economic society are being inculcated. The process of economic education for good or ill goes on continually both in school and out. This view is expressed by A. J. Stoddard, who writes:

> It [economic education] is necessary [beginning in the kindergarten] because economic habits, values, concepts, and opinions, like health habits and beliefs, do not wait for a particular school grade or level of maturity. In short, economic education will take place in these early years whether or not we provide it. [34:27]

George Coe, inquiring how children come under the control of economic forces and how they acquire economic consciousness, points out in his book, *Law and Freedom in the Schools,* that such facts as the following come very early into the circle of the child's experience: the dependence of satisfactions upon money; the sources of the family income; the distinction between employing and being employed; the existence of poverty; social distinctions based on income or possessions;

the economic conception of success; and the prestige of wealth. [7:106] Through environmental pressure the child learns the ideas and attitudes that prevail in our economic life. Unfortunately, many of these ideas and attitudes are too individualistic to be suited to modern conditions. They have outlived their usefulness. Yet they will be perpetuated so long as the child's economic education is undirected. The power of economic tradition to shape the young is thus described by Coe:

These economic forces and laws, operative under the eyes of everyone, yet not fully avowed, and never put into textbooks, constitute one of the most stupendous of all educative forces. Silently, unnoticed by the child or by his elders, the young mind bends into conformity to the system. It is taken for granted because it is omnipresent and practically un-challenged. Moreover, it seems to be a thing of nature, for indeed it appeals to native traits, such as getting, accumulating, holding, emulating, mastering, admiration for power, and fondness for being admired. It makes, likewise, another profound appeal—to our fears. To be sure to have enough, and to provide against contingencies for one's self and for one's children—such contingencies as unemployment, sickness, old age, low prices or high prices—all this seems as natural as seizing food when one is hungry. Thus, in short, *the system as it is* impresses itself upon the young as both natural and right, as natural law and moral law combined. [7:110]

It is clear that if education for economic competence is to fulfill its functions—particularly in the area of economic citizenship—it cannot be postponed to adulthood or even to adolescence. The competence necessary to bring our economic system under democratic control requires new thought-patterns, which must be learned before the young mind has been too thoroughly impressed by old traditions.

CHAPTER TWO

Purpose and Procedures of the Study

LITTLE is known concerning what the elementary schools are doing or might do to educate for economic competence. The purpose of this investigation is to explore what is being done.

PREVIOUS STUDIES

Previous studies that throw light on the place of education for economic competence in the elementary school fall into two classes: (1) studies of the curriculum based on analyses of textbooks, courses of study, or questionnaire reports from school administrators; and (2) studies of the out-of-school experiences of children. The number of studies in either class is small.

Nearly all the studies in the first group have been confined to a few school systems and cover only a small part of the subject. They deal mainly with instruction in thrift, foods, clothing, or consumer-business practices. There are, however, three comprehensive analyses of the elementary curriculum which contain data useful in determining the status of education for economic competence in the first six grades. These will be briefly outlined.

Carey, Hanna, and Meriam in 1932 catalogued 7,000 units of work, activities, and projects described in professional books, courses of study, pamphlets, and periodicals published for the most part between January 1, 1925, and December 31, 1931. The index of this catalogue demonstrates that the activity curriculum is rich in experiences at least potentially significant for economic education. Each item is indexed once, under its principal theme. Under "transportation" 143 titles are listed; under "store," 135; under "farming," 120; under "clothing," 65; under "poultry," 25; under "toys," 20; under "thrift," 20; under "market,"

18

17; under "money," 8; and so on.[1] Obviously, such units might be taught so as to contribute to economic competence.

H. B. Bruner tabulated the major topics in recent social studies courses for grades four, five, and six, using a nation-wide sampling with an average of forty courses per grade. He found the number of courses in which a given broad topic, such as "manufacturing," "housing," "clothing," or "cereals," appears as a unit title or major heading of a unit. How the broad topics are developed, and whether they are so treated as to bring out their implications for economic competence, cannot be determined from the published data, but it is clear that many of the topics have important economic bearing.[2]

Henry Harap indexed 391 separate units in eighty-nine activity curricula published between 1919 and 1938. Most of the curriculum materials consist of course of study bulletins, but some are books of units or series of units in pamphlet form issued by commercial publishers. The units are indexed according to their central theme or themes. By consulting the index one can find, for example, that fifty of the units deal with buying and selling things, thirty-three each with farming and transportation, twenty with clothing, two with textiles, two with insuring life and property, one with shoes, and so on. A large number of the units treat phases of economic life.[3]

The second group of studies—those of the out-of-school experiences of children—are, like the first group, few in number, and for the most part concerned with but a small fragment of the child's experiences.

The most comprehensive study is that made by Florence O'Neil and Mary McCormick. It presents the home duties and health behavior of 3,512 children, as reported by parents in an interview with the children's teacher.[4] The findings show that 50 per cent of the boys and 75 per cent of the girls of eight, nine, and ten years of age helped prepare and serve meals; 59 per cent of the boys and 87 per cent of the girls of eleven, twelve, and thirteen years of age had this home duty. The

[1] Carey, Alice E., Hanna, Paul R., Meriam, J. L., *Catalog: Units of Work, Activities, Projects, etc.* 1932.

[2] Bruner, H. B., *What Our Schools Are Teaching.* 1941.

[3] Harap, Henry, *An Index to Units in Eighty-Nine Activity Curricula.* 1938.

[4] O'Neil, Florence C. and McCormick, Mary G., *Everyday Behavior of Elementary School Children: Report of a Study of the Twenty-Four-Hour Day Health Behavior of 3512 Individual Children.* University of the State of New York, 1934.

diet of most of the children was found inadequate; for instance, 75 per cent had less than a quart of milk a day, and 20 per cent had little or no milk, while one-third had green-leaf vegetables less than twice weekly.

Dorothy Warren and W. H. Burton had 1,000 fifth and sixth graders mark a check list of the consumer-business practices which they had often, seldom, or never experienced. It was found that the children were experiencing often or seldom most of the business practices reported by twenty-five adults who kept a record of their consumer-business activities for two weeks.[5]

Sister Mary de Paul Gillette studied the buying practices of 3,170 children in grades one through eight. These children were asked to record all articles purchased during a period of one week, the instructions which they received, and what they would like to know about buying. Most of the children were doing a considerable amount of buying of food, and reported many anxieties in connection with this shopping.[6]

Reseda Payne made an intensive study of the buying experiences of 81 Negro girls in the fifth and sixth grades of a school in an underprivileged area of Cincinnati. In one-half of the homes of these girls, the mothers were gainfully employed. Two-thirds of the girls were doing practically all the marketing for the home.[7]

Sara Chase studied the buying experiences of 209 children in the fourth, fifth, and sixth grades of a school in Springfield, Massachusetts. The children in one month made 4,209 trips to stores and purchased 152 commodities of a total value of $1,246.[8]

Edgar Dale noted the purchases made by 166 children at a grocery store. Most of the children were estimated to be from seven to ten years

[5] Warren, Dorothy and Burton, W. H., "Knowledge of Simple Business Practices Possessed by Intermediate Grade Pupils." *Elementary School Journal*, Vol. 35, pp. 511–16, March, 1935.

[6] Gillette, Sister Mary de Paul, O.P., "A Plan to Enrich the Curricula of a Group of Elementary and Secondary Parochial Schools to Meet the Interests and Needs of Pupils with Respect to Buying Goods." Unpublished Doctor of Education thesis, Teachers College, Columbia University. 1936.

[7] Payne, Reseda B., "Investigation into the Buying Experiences of Fifth and Sixth Grade Girls at Jackson School." Unpublished Master's thesis, University of Cincinnati. 1932.

[8] Chase, Sara E., "Individual Differences in the Experience of Children." Unpublished Master's thesis, University of Chicago. 1927.

of age. Seventy-five per cent of the purchases amounted to less than fifty cents.[9]

Questionnaires filled out for Gavian by 95 children in grades four through eight showed that nearly all the children did considerable buying of groceries, school needs, gifts, and small items of clothing, and that practically all had earned money.[10]

Knowledge of children's home duties, health behavior, and consumer-business experiences is useful in planning the elementary curriculum to meet the immediate needs of the children. The studies cited support the opinion that education for economic competence is desirable in the elementary grades.

NEED FOR THIS INVESTIGATION

No comprehensive investigation of the economic content of the elementary curriculum has ever been made. No one has explored the question of what the elementary schools are doing to lay a foundation for economic competence in later years. There is need for an exploratory investigation of education for economic competence in the first six grades. Such an exploration should serve to open up the field for other investigators. Information to be obtained from this and subsequent studies should make possible the strengthening of the elementary curriculum with respect to aims, materials, and methods in educating for economic competence. The information should also be of interest to secondary school curriculum workers who are concerned with making education more functional and obtaining better vertical integration between the elementary and secondary curricula.

ASSUMPTIONS AND THESES

The present study rests on three major assumptions:

1. That education for economic competence should constitute a substantial part of the education of children.

[9] Dale, Edgar, "Economics for Children." *Educational Research Bulletin*, Vol. IX, No. 14, pp. 381–84, October 8, 1930.
[10] Gavian, Ruth Wood, "Children's Experiences with Money." *Social Education*, Vol. II, pp. 166–68, March, 1938.

2. That the school's part of the task of education for economic competence must begin and does begin in the first six grades.

3. That the strengthening of the work of the elementary school in educating for economic competence depends upon clarification of the aims, and discovery of the materials and methods best suited to realizing the aims.

The principal theses of this study are as follows:

1. Many of the topics commonly treated in the first six grades and many of the activities commonly carried on in these grades may be the vehicles for learnings which have a significant relation to economic competence.

2. A minority of course of study writers are already aware of the implications of these topics and activities for economic competence.

SELECTION OF A METHOD OF INVESTIGATION

To determine the present status of education for economic competence in the first six grades, seven methods might conceivably be used. Considerations which led to the rejection of six of the methods and the selection of the seventh are noted below.

1. Testing of samples of the elementary school population to determine achievement with respect to the skills and understandings involved in economic competence. This is an investigation which should assuredly be made, but to carry it out adequately would require the labor of a number of experts in testing over a considerable period of time. The necessary setup would be comparable to that of the study of character education made by Hartshorne, May, and Shuttleworth.[11] Before such a study could be made it would be necessary to discover what the schools are trying to do in this area, inasmuch as outcomes can be measured only in terms of objectives.

2. Questionnaires addressed to a sampling of elementary school teachers, asking their objectives and practices in this area. These might be supplemented by questionnaires addressed to parents, asking their opinion of what the schools to which their children go are accomplish-

[11] Hartshorne, Hugh, May, Mark A., and Shuttleworth, F. K., *Studies in the Nature of Character.* 3v. Character Education Inquiry, Teachers College, Columbia University. Macmillan, 1928.

ing with respect to education for economic competence. The usual limitations of the questionnaire method would be accentuated in investigating an area as broad and difficult to define as that of the present study. The questionnaire method might, however, be used to advantage in investigating some one segment of education for economic competence, such as education in the selection of clothing or education with respect to local occupations.

3. Interviews with teachers, possibly supplemented by interviews with parents and children, to find out what is being taught in the area of education for economic competence. Experiments in interviewing teachers made by the investigator indicate that the area of education for economic competence is far too broad to be explored effectively by this method.

4. Classroom observations in a few selected schools. The amount of data that could be gathered by one investigator in a limited period did not appear to warrant the use of this method. Unless one observed the work of teachers who are particularly interested in educating for economic competence, the data obtained would be meager.

5. Analysis of textbooks. This method is of little use in exploring curriculum content in the primary grades, where a large part of the teaching is incidental to activities. The method is better adapted to getting at curriculum content in the intermediate grades, where the textbooks used commonly determine most of the curriculum. However, even in a textbook-dominated curriculum there is likely to be incidental teaching of such topics as the selection of a good school lunch, appropriate clothing, care of clothing, and thrift in buying, particularly if these topics are emphasized in the course of study.

6. Analysis of published or unpublished units of work. The analysis of manuscript reports of units of work collected by certain state departments of education was seriously considered. The investigator read one hundred and fifty manuscript reports of social studies units collected by the Bureau of Curriculum Development of the New York State Department of Education. The schools sending these units had been released from all the requirements of the state social studies syllabus. Although some of the units were highly original, it was found that except for organization many did not vary substantially from the materials of the syllabus, and that most of the units on any one topic,

such as "Indians," covered much the same ground by means of much the same activities. This experience in reading manuscript units suggested that data could be gathered more quickly and economically by analyzing courses of study.

7. Analysis of a sampling of courses of study. The principal limitation of this method is the uncertainty as to the extent to which the work of teachers is actually reflected in or influenced by the course of study. Do the printed objectives reflect those of the typical teacher? If not, does the typical teacher read or adopt them? If she does not adopt them in entirety, does acquaintance with them influence her work? There is similar doubt as to whether the subject matter outlined in the course of study is the content actually taught. Does the typical teacher in planning her work take over the subject matter of the course of study in whole or in part? Does she gather together her own subject matter? Does she depend upon the children to obtain it from a basal textbook? Or does she allow them to gather it more or less at random from whatever books are available? The answers to these questions are not known and might profitably be investigated.

In the absence of any proof of the extent to which courses of study either reflect or influence the objectives of teachers and the subject matter that is taught, certain facts as to the nature of courses of study should be taken into account.

Courses of study, especially those of recent date, are extremely diverse. Some contain a graded list of topics suitable for large units, and by reporting units actually taught show how these topics may be developed. Warning is always given that these reports are not to be copied in detail.[12] Another group of course of study bulletins containing reports of actual units differs from those described above in that no sequence and scope of subject matter is indicated. Presumably these reports represent the best current practices known to the compilers. Publications of this type are exemplified by the Michigan bulletin No. 306, *Instructional Practices in Elementary Schools,* and the Tennessee bulletin, *Looking Ahead with Tennessee Schools.*[13]

[12] The frequent occurrence of these warnings must mean that the writers believe that teachers are inclined to follow the courses too closely.

[13] Bulletins of this type were not used in the analysis of courses of study to be hereinafter described. Inasmuch as no scope and sequence is given, they could not be analyzed on the same check lists with bulletins having a definite scope and sequence.

A large proportion of courses of study contain detailed subject-matter outlines—"ground to be covered." In many cases they are designed to be used in connection with state-adopted textbooks, some merely outlining the material in the designated basal text. Since the use of a basal text determines the curriculum in large measure, it follows that a course of study built on the use of a designated basal text will bear a close relation to actual classroom practice. Some courses of study containing subject-matter outlines do not recommend the use of any particular basal text; they may even suggest that the teacher exercise freedom in deciding which parts of the outlined subject matter she will emphasize or use. A few give the teacher a choice not only of subject matter, but even of the large units to be taught. The Madison, Wisconsin, courses in science and social studies are of this type.

Whatever the relationship may be between a given course of study and classroom practice in the place to which it is meant to apply, that relationship is conditioned by: (1) the nature of the course of study— its philosophy, objectives, recency, helpfulness to teachers, whether or not it is designed for use with a basal text, and whether or not a choice of subject matter is offered; (2) the procedures by which the course was compiled and promulgated, and the proportion of the teachers expected to use it who helped in producing it; (3) its availability. Recent courses vary so much with respect to these factors that one can hardly assert that as a whole they either do or do not indicate what is actually going on in the schools. At the least they show what school administrators wish to have going on in their respective jurisdictions.

For the purposes of this particular research, the investigator concluded that the analysis of courses of study offered fewer difficulties and limitations than any other method.

METHODS USED IN ANALYZING THE COURSES OF STUDY

Questions to Be Answered

It was decided to analyze a sample of elementary courses of study for the purpose of finding the answers to four questions:

1. What objectives bearing on economic competence are stated?
2. What are the commonly occurring topics and activities most

likely to be the vehicles for learnings having a significant relation to economic competence?

3. In how many courses and on which grade levels does each topic or activity appear at least once?

4. What materials related to each topic and likely to contribute to economic competence can be found in the courses of study?

SELECTION OF THE COURSES OF STUDY

Because the demand for increased attention to economic education was only beginning to be prominent in the early 1930's, it was decided to analyze no courses published before January 1, 1930. This plan was adhered to except in a few cases where, in order to improve the geographic distribution of the sampling, it seemed advisable to add one or two courses of earlier date.

Four samples were prepared: (1) general courses (a general course is one that includes in one volume all the different subjects to be taught); (2) social studies courses, including a small number of separate courses in geography and history; (3) science or nature study courses; and (4) arithmetic courses.

In selecting courses for analysis, state courses were preferred to city and county courses. Every general, social studies, science, or arithmetic course published by any state since January 1, 1930, was used, if a copy could be found in the Teachers College curriculum laboratory. The only exceptions were courses that indicated no scope and sequence of subject matter, and those that consisted of little more than general remarks and a list of adopted textbooks.

When the available state courses were too few, so that some sections of the United States were not represented in the sample, city or county courses were chosen, practically at random, to represent these areas. The city courses chosen come from cities of all sizes. The few county courses represent both rural and urban counties. It is believed that each of the four samples represents a good geographic distribution of courses published in the United States since the beginning of 1930. The Southeast is less fully represented in the samples of social studies, arithmetic, and science courses than are the other areas, presumably because not many new courses have been published in this section since 1930.

The size and composition of the four samples are as follows:

GENERAL COURSES[14]
  State courses, 168
  County courses, 20
  City courses, 22
  Total, 210 courses (or 35 for each grade from one through six)
  Population of the areas covered by the courses, 65,000,000

ARITHMETIC COURSES
  State courses, 39
  County courses, 3
  City courses, 72
  Total, 114 courses (or 38 for each grade from four through six)
  Population of the areas covered by the courses, 49,000,000

SOCIAL STUDIES COURSES
  State courses, 76
  County courses, 9
  City courses, 125
  Total, 210 courses (or 35 for each grade from one through six)
  Population of the areas covered by the courses, 48,000,000

SCIENCE COURSES
  State courses, 60
  County courses, 12
  City courses, 66
  Total, 138 courses (or 23 for each grade from one through six)
  Population of the areas covered by the courses, 43,000,000

THE STATEMENTS OF OBJECTIVES

The statements of philosophy, aims, objectives, or desired outcomes found in the four samples of courses of study were read, and the items bearing on education for economic competence were entered upon cards. The range and number of items thus gathered were small, and the samples were supplemented by additional curriculum bulletins[15] until it appeared that further additions would yield nothing of importance to the study. The objectives were then classified and examples chosen to illustrate each category. The findings are presented in Chapter Three.

SELECTION OF THE TOPICS

An attempt was made to list those frequently occurring topics most likely to carry learnings that have a significant bearing on economic competence. The steps in selecting the topics in social studies and general courses were as follows:

[14] The word "course," as used on this page and throughout the book, refers to material designed for use in a single grade. A general course is a complete program for a grade, while a social studies, arithmetic, or science course is only part of the program.

[15] The word "bulletin" is used in this book to indicate any publication on the curriculum issued by school authorities. A bulletin usually contains a number of courses, but it may include only one course or none.

1. Seven major headings were listed under which it was expected that the topics would fall, and some of the principal learnings related to economic competence that might be looked for under each major heading were noted.

2. Several complete courses of study for the first six grades were read and the topics which carried the learnings related to economic competence noted. Certain topics expected to occur in other courses were added, among them "cooperatives," "government-owned business," "how to use consumer credit," "unemployment," and "how a private enterprise is organized and managed." In this way a tentative list of eighty topics was drawn up.

3. A check list was prepared on which to record the occurrence of each topic in each course of study. As the reading and checking of courses proceeded, topics were occasionally encountered that were not on the list. It was usually possible to combine a new topic with one already listed; in this case the written description was expanded to include the new item. Thus the item "lighting and heating a home" was added to the topic "home care and improvement," and the item "inspection of food stores and dairies" was added to the topic "health protection in the local community." A new topic that could not be combined with an old one was noted, but it was not added to the check list unless it was found in bulletins from more than two places.

4. As the checking of the courses proceeded, it was seen that a few of the original topics were not sufficiently well defined to be easily recognized, and that certain others were restricted to the arithmetic section of general courses. These were eliminated. After the analysis was completed, the topics which had been found in courses from fewer than three places were listed separately. (See Table VIII, p. 146.) Fifty-six topics were left and these are presented in Tables I to VII.

A somewhat different procedure was followed in selecting the topics from the arithmetic and science courses. A tentative list of topics was not made out in advance, but during the reading of the courses, each topic that appeared to contribute to economic competence was, when encountered for the first time, noted on the tabulation sheet. Each new item was separately listed on the check list instead of being combined with some related item. The topics found in arithmetic and science courses are presented in Tables IX to XII.

PROCEDURE FOLLOWED IN COUNTING THE TOPICS

In the process of reading courses of study and entering upon the check list the topics found, the following procedures were observed.

1. Items found in a course were entered in one check list only. Arithmetic, social studies, or science items found in an outline in a general course of study were entered only in the general check list. They were not used for the arithmetic, social studies, or science check lists.

2. A topic was checked only once for each grade, regardless of how many times it might appear in the course of study for that grade.

3. Topics found in objectives, generalizations, or desired outcomes listed in the introductory matter of a bulletin or a course were not entered in the check list. If, however, a topic was found in the objectives, generalizations, or desired outcomes of a particular unit it was entered whether or not it occurred elsewhere in the unit.

4. A topic was entered in the check list even though it appeared only in a subject-matter outline, in a list of suggested activities, in a list of generalizations that might be developed, or in a list of subjects for reports. As a rule, however, the same topic appeared in two or more of these places, and often in the objectives or desired outcomes as well.[16]

5. When a topic was not definitely placed in a course for a single grade, but was recommended for several grades, e.g., for grades 1 to 3 or grades 4 to 6, it was entered in the check list for each of the grades named.

6. A topic was considered to be present in a course of study even though it was represented only by one of its sub-topics. "Learning to clean shoes" was checked against the topic "Care of clothing"; "Learning about the post office" was checked against the topic "Communication"; "Learning the value of milk as a food" was checked against "Selecting a healthful diet"; "Visiting a bakery to observe the process of making bread" was checked against "Manufacturing." This procedure made it possible to keep the list of topics at a length that would be manageable.

[16] At the outset an attempt was made to distinguish by symbols between topics that are merely suggestive and those that the course of study writer regarded as essential. In practice it proved impossible to maintain any clear-cut distinction between these two categories.

RELIABILITY OF THE PROCEDURE

In order to check on the accuracy of the counting, three experienced elementary teachers were asked to count topics in a few social studies, science, or arithmetic courses. These had already been analyzed by the investigator and were selected for rechecking because of their brevity. The checkers received the list of topics then being used in analyzing courses of each type, and after brief preliminary instructions and the counting of topics in one course for practice, proceeded to count topics in additional courses without assistance. Each of five science courses, four arithmetic courses, and five social studies courses were covered by two checkers. Each checker spent about three hours on the counting.

It is obvious that the practice period was much too brief to allow the checkers to memorize the list of topics and to learn to recognize the many verbal patterns in which the topics are expressed. It was to be expected, therefore, that many items would be missed.

In each case where a topic counted by a checker had not previously been counted by the investigator, the course was re-examined. In some cases the mention was of a merely passing nature, e.g., "farming" in the sentence "Farming is the leading industry of the South," and was accordingly rejected. In other cases, where the topic found by the checker was clearly intended to be developed, it was added to the investigator's original count for that course.

In five science courses the investigator had missed 16 per cent on the average of the topics ultimately listed for each course. In five social studies courses the investigator had missed 10.9 per cent on the average of the topics ultimately listed for each course. In four arithmetic courses the investigator had missed 2.7 per cent on the average of the topics ultimately listed for each course.

Later the investigator repeated the analysis of a Mississippi general course of study which had been made seven months earlier. Whereas some six hours had been spent in the original analysis of this 582-page volume, the use of a skimming technique during the second analysis reduced the time by one-half. In comparing results, it was found that six per cent of the items counted on the first reading were missed on the second, while less than one per cent of those counted on the second had been missed on the first.

The missing of topics seems readily explainable by the fact that in the counting one is strongly inclined merely to skim rather than to read carefully. As a result some items are overlooked.

SELECTION OF MATERIALS TO ILLUSTRATE CONTENT OF FIFTY-SIX TOPICS

In order to show how each of the fifty-six topics found in social studies and general courses may serve as a vehicle for learnings having significant relation to economic competence, it was decided to collect from the courses analyzed materials in which these learnings are made explicit.

The method used in gathering these materials was as follows: In reading each course of study the investigator watched for problems and activities which seemed to have a definite bearing on economic competence. When such an item was found it was copied on a small card, together with the name of the bulletin, the grade level, and the page. The card was filed under the topic to which the item was most closely related. The same item appearing in another course of study was not copied, unless it was more fully developed or unless it brought out more clearly the economic learning involved.

After all the materials had been collected, those related to each topic were read. In a few cases the same item had been copied from two courses of study. Other items appeared to have rather slight significance for economic competence. These were discarded. The remainder are presented in Chapter Four.

SUMMARY OF THE FINDINGS

Courses of study and other curriculum bulletins were searched for statements of philosophy and aims which might bear upon education for economic competence. Fifteen distinct objectives were found. These are listed on pp. 34–5.

Analysis of 420 general and social studies courses[17] produced a list of fifty-six topics, found in courses from more than two places, about which the learnings related to economic competence appear to cluster. The median item was found in 20 per cent of the courses. The topics fall into seven groups, which are listed here with the percentage of courses in which the average topic of the group appeared at least once:

I. Industries and occupations in the modern world (38%). II. Home life in our community (30%). III. Conservation (28%). IV. Local community services and their support (20%). V. Characteristics of a machine civilization (15%). VI. Money management (7%). VII. Business organization; banking (4%).

In arithmetic courses for grades four through six were found forty-seven topics in courses from more than two places that seemed likely to carry learnings related to economic competence. The median item appears in only 8 per cent of the courses analyzed. This low frequency may be attributed to the neglect of the informational content of the subject in most arithmetic courses for intermediate grades.

In science courses fifty-three topics likely to carry learnings contributory to economic competence were found in courses from more than two places, the median item appearing in 13 per cent of the courses. Almost the only topics that occur frequently are those related to conservation. A few courses in the sample consistently relate scientific principles to the affairs of the household and the farm, but little attention is given in any of them to the selection of foods and to community problems of health, housing, and diet.

Samples of course of study materials likely to contribute to education for economic competence, and related to each of the fifty-six topics found in general and social studies courses, are presented in Chapter Four. While some of these materials are designated for use on a lower grade level than may prove most advantageous for their initial presentation to children, the collection supports two conclusions: (1) that the potential contribution of the elementary school to education for economic competence is large; and (2) that some existing courses of study, particularly in social studies, contain a wide variety of economic problems and activities that appear, on the whole, to be adapted to the interests and abilities of children in the first six grades.

[17] The word "course" is used to mean the program for a single grade.

CHAPTER THREE

Objectives Bearing on
Economic Competence

THE first problem to be dealt with in the present investigation is: "What objectives bearing on economic competence are stated in elementary courses of study?"

Many curriculum bulletins, especially those of the more traditional types, contain no statement of philosophy or aims. In those which do, the types of statement vary enormously. Some are very brief, others very lengthy. The more elaborate include lists of abilities, habits, attitudes, appreciations, and generalizations to be developed. Sometimes the word "objective" is replaced by the term "desired outcome." For purposes of this inquiry these terms will be used interchangeably.

PROCEDURE

Each course of study in the four samples (general, social studies, science, and arithmetic) was searched for statements of philosophy and aims. Any item in such a statement which appeared to have a significant bearing on education for economic competence was copied on a card.

Since the number and range of items in the bulletins included in the samples were rather limited, it seemed advisable to use additional bulletins. Several state education departments had issued more recent curriculum publications than the course of study by which their state is represented in the sample, and these yielded a number of new items. Many tentative courses of study and reports of social studies committees engaged in curriculum revision in New York communities, on file in the State Department of Education at Albany, were also searched,

33

but few new items were found. It seemed unlikely that examination of other curriculum bulletins would add anything important.

The items that had been gathered were then sorted. Those that related to specific practical abilities, e. g., to compute interest, or to select a well-balanced lunch, were discarded. The remaining items were studied to discover what groupings would most accurately reflect the intent of the writers with respect to education for economic competence.

CLASSIFICATION OF THE OBJECTIVES

It is believed that all the objectives found can be classified, without violence to their writers' intent, under the following scheme:

The Elementary School should develop:

1. Social-economic orientation.
2. Occupational orientation.
3. Understanding of social-economic problems.
4. An attitude of hospitality toward needed social-economic change.
5. An interest in, the democratic planning of social-economic change.
6. Awareness of the place of the machine in our civilization, and the possibilities inherent in mass production.
7. Awareness of the struggle for economic democracy.
8. Awareness of the adaptations demanded by an increasingly interdependent economy:
   a. A more cooperative and less individualistic society.
   b. Greater economic cooperation between nations.
   c. Assumption by the community of the responsibility to provide the necessaries of life when the individual cannot provide them for himself.
   d. Support and use of an increasing variety of community and government services.
9. Understanding of the importance of conserving human and material resources including natural beauty.
10. Thrift and intelligent money management, including appreciation of what parents have to spend.
11. Ability to make wise selection and use of goods and services.

12. An interest in the use of tax money.
13. Knowledge of productive processes by which individuals, families, and communities may increase their real incomes.
14. Knowledge of common business terms and practices.
15. Understanding of some of the basic vocabulary of economics.

This composite statement of objectives includes most of the items listed on pp. 8–10 as essential to economic competence. In the following pages each of the fifteen objectives will be illustrated with excerpts from courses of study and other curriculum bulletins.

1. SOCIAL-ECONOMIC ORIENTATION

The need of orienting the elementary pupil to the social-economic relationships of the people and things about him is brought out in an Arkansas* curriculum bulletin. Note that the terms "social experience," and "social environment" are evidently intended to include the economic aspects:

The pupil coming to school from the average home knows little of the fundamental social and economic life in which he participates. It is the function of the school to orient the pupil in his social setting by providing social experiences adapted to his level of development. As he experiences successive contacts, the individual will progressively develop a deeper understanding of the life about him and the relationships between the various aspects of his social environment. [39:16]

The same idea is expressed in the Denver program in social studies for primary grades:

The average home is no longer able to give the child instruction in economic and social living. Children must be given help in sensing and understanding the social relationships bound up in their everyday experiences. [127:13–14]

That social-economic orientation begins in the first years of school is also pointed out in a recent Los Angeles curriculum bulletin:

The primary school is an arranged environment which initiates the child through first-hand experiences into actual practice of certain important human activities that are significant in his life from birth to death. . . .

* Whenever a course of study or curriculum bulletin is designated by the name of a state rather than of a city or county, it is an official publication of the state department of education or public instruction.

The school orients each child into appropriate and safe use of many kinds of materials and equipment, helps him to understand, as a part of his personal experiences, some of the problems of property rights, protection of property, and the conservation of property. . . . It extends his concepts into socio-economic realities, including simple processes and the uses and significances of modern communication and transportation. [51:54]

A desired outcome in the Oregon course of study in elementary arithmetic is "a realistic understanding of the operation of economic factors." [103:71a] A criterion for selecting a social studies activity, according to a Utah bulletin, is that "the activity chosen should enrich the child's understanding of and appreciation for the social, political, and economic life of his community." [191:iii]

2. OCCUPATIONAL ORIENTATION

The need for orienting the child to the adult world of work is stated in a considerable number of the elementary courses examined. One general aim of the elementary school, according to a Springfield, Massachusetts, bulletin on social studies, is "to develop vocational understanding through a study of occupations." [190:Introduction] Similarly, a Michigan bulletin declares:

Although specific vocational training is not considered as an aim of elementary education, it is desirable through field trips and exploratory experiences to give an introduction to vocational life. [54:12]

Where many children do not continue in school beyond the elementary period, it is natural that occupational orientation should be emphasized. The Kentucky state course of study expresses this idea:

It will be well during this [fifth] grade to make selections that will describe the occupations of the various industries. If they are to be placed in the proper work in life, pupils must begin to learn at this age what are the requirements of the various industries. [49:229]

In many curriculum bulletins occupational units are designated for the first or second grade. The Fort Worth program in social studies provides for the second grade a unit half a year in length entitled, "How the work of the community is carried on." Among the desired outcomes are: knowledge and understanding of community workers and their occupations, the training required for each, appreciation of the dignity of labor and of the benefits derived from these workers, and an attitude of respect and tolerance for them. Further, "It is hoped that the child will become conscious of the fact that he must become a worker and begin to observe all types of workers at their work." [132:29] Similar objectives are given in a South Dakota unit for the second grade. [187:119]

Recognition of the fact that attitudes toward work begin to be built up early in life is found in a number of elementary bulletins. Thus the Virginia elementary curriculum program includes as desired outcomes the following emotionalized attitudes: appreciation of good workmanship, the feeling of the worth of the man whose work is marked by integrity, the sense of the value of technical skill, the capacity to enjoy the precision of a great organization. [73:7]

The Springfield, Massachusetts, program in social studies for intermediate grades seeks "appreciation of the interdependence of capital and labor." [190:166] A similar outcome desired in the Detroit social studies program is "to appreciate the importance of sympathetic cooperation between capital and labor." [131:269] An objective of a Hartford, Connecticut, bulletin on social studies is appreciation of the "desirability of employment under any conditions in preference to idleness." [135:44] If the implications of this statement appear somewhat ominous, they are perhaps counterbalanced by those of a generalization-to-be-developed in the Alabama curriculum that "An individual has the right to earn a living for himself and his family." [223:53]

The Grand Rapids bulletin on social studies for kindergarten and first grade declares: "The child should come to a realization that it is self-respecting and satisfying to earn what is received." [134:1] Among "truths which the small child can gradually understand," this publication states: "Sometimes it is the woman's job to do the housework and sometimes it is the father's; either should be respected if he does his work well." [134:17]

The excerpts given above are typical of others indicating a concern on the part of a number of curriculum writers that the elementary school shall develop in the child the proper attitude toward workers and toward work. For the most part the attitudes sought are those sanctioned by tradition; rarely is it suggested that new attitudes may be demanded in adjusting to modern conditions.

3. Understanding of Social-Economic Problems

Like adults, children seem to have a natural interest in those aspects of social relationships which are unsettled, and particularly those which involve conflict. While the desirability of cultivating this interest is not discussed in the majority of the elementary courses of study examined, there are a few which declare emphatically that social-economic problems should be considered in the elementary grades. An illustration is found in the South Dakota bulletin on intermediate social studies:

The American people today are confronted with many problems or issues which are not only affecting their mode of living and the present and future welfare of their natural life but which are also demanding solution for the people of this generation and those that follow.

The contribution of the schools to the solution of these problems has been, and is, almost negligible. It has been assumed that little could be done about many of these problems, particularly in the grade schools, since obviously it would be unwise and inappropriate to present to pupils of the elementary age abstract theories regarding our major political, social, and economic problems. Many of these problems, however, have certain phases that are within the experience of elementary children and that can be discussed and understood with great profit. [188:21]

A similar statement is taken from the Colorado course of study for elementary schools:

That we have not understood our social environment and have not been able to control it, is becoming more obvious each year. . . . This course of study provides suggestions through which teachers and pupils can study their social environment and arrive at a better understanding of the social order of which they are a part.

While it is not expected that elementary pupils will be able to appreciate fully the more involved social and economic problems, it is believed that the understandings and attitudes gained through an impartial presentation of these things will contribute to a public opinion necessary for social improvement. [41:4]

According to the Fort Worth course in social studies for the sixth grade, "The curriculum should reflect the social, political, and economic problems of the modern world." [132:3] The same idea was repeated four years later in the Fort Worth course in mathematics for intermediate grades: "The curriculum should consider definitely the problems of economic, political, social, and individual life." [88:iv]

One of the objectives of the Kansas program in social studies is:

To develop an appreciation and an understanding of important present-day problems, and the responsibility of pupils to participate in the solution of present-day and future problems. [163:19]

That the public schools should be concerned with the problems of the local community is the theme of a recent elementary curriculum bulletin issued at Glencoe, Illinois:

In community education, adults as well as children co-operate in the continuous improvement of the basic functions of human living. The activities and problems of the immediate community will constitute increasingly the source of learning experiences. [44:2]

4. An Attitude of Hospitality toward Needed Social-Economic Change

The following excerpt from a Michigan bulletin for elementary schools illustrates this objective:

If education is to progress, pupils and teachers alike must develop an attitude that is favorable to change and improvement. Boys and girls must learn to expect that society will continue to find better solutions for old problems. [54:13]

A generalization-to-be-developed, according to an Alabama bulletin, is: "Man continues to modify the present social order in his search for freedom and justice." [223:53]

5. An Interest in the Democratic Planning of Social-Economic Change

Intelligent modification of the social order depends on social-economic planning. To create an interest in such planning is an implied objective of a few elementary courses. One example, found in a San Mateo County, California, bulletin and credited to Dr. John C. Almack of Stanford University, follows:

Outline for Organizing the Social Studies

1. What we have today:	1. at home and in the community
2. What we had yesterday:	2. in the state and the nation
3. What we should have tomorrow:	3. in other lands [185:4]

The question, "What should we have tomorrow?" is basic to social-economic planning and implies that one task of the social studies is to interest boys and girls in the democratic planning of social-economic change. Another example, from the Houston social studies course, appears under the heading "An interest in the use of tax money," on page 49 of this study.

6. Awareness of the Place of the Machine in Our Civilization and the Possibilities Inherent in Mass Production

That our people do not see clearly as yet the changes in social relationships brought about by the machine and do not realize the possibilities for good and for evil inherent in machine production, is plain. In the last decade curriculum makers have begun to try to remedy this shortage. While the importance of beginning in the elementary school to build the necessary understandings is being recognized, this objective is explicit in only a small proportion of elementary courses of study.

Generalizations and appreciations bearing on the place of the machine in our civilization may be found in nearly every unit of the Houston program in social studies for elementary grades. In a unit for third grade, the following are sought:

(1) Appreciation of the fact that the increased use of machines in production has enabled us to have more things at a cheaper price than would have been possible without them. (2) Appreciation of how the use of machines has tended toward a greater specialization of labor, and has, in turn, helped bring about a vast chain of interdependence of mankind everywhere. [138:3]

In a Houston unit for fifth grade appears the generalization-to-be-developed:

In all ages past, culture has rested upon slavery and exploitation; in the present age and in the future it may rest largely upon the use of machines, which release large numbers from drudgery. [148:1]

A California committee on the elementary curriculum has suggested for fifth and sixth grades, units on how man's life has been changed by the machine; farming in modern times; the history of records, travel, lighting, electricity, and communication. Miss Helen Heffernan, a member of the committee, writes:

In the development of these units the teacher is not only helping the child to acquire an interesting body of information, but she is attempting to give him insight into the fact that the exercise of technological controls has brought in its wake serious problems of social and economic adjustment, and that the machine does not necessarily mean progress unless it can be utilized for the welfare of all mankind rather than debased for purposes of human exploitation. [16:21]

The Virginia core curriculum places great emphasis on understanding the place of the machine, designating as the center of interest for the sixth grade, "The effects of machine production upon our living." Among the understandings to be developed are:

(1) Machine production tends to increase the interdependence of groups, to lighten man's labor, to increase opportunities for recreation and creative expression, to furnish a greater variety and different quality of goods, to force the application of scientific methods to social problems; (2) Mass production increases the wealth of the few; (3) Mass production operated solely for personal gain tends to produce poverty, vice, and disease; (4) Man must learn to control his discoveries and invention. [73:180–1]

Most of these understandings on the effect of machine production listed in the Virginia course of study are quoted in the Hamilton County (Tennessee) Yearbook for 1936–37 as objectives for a sixth grade unit, "How Our Country Grew." [45:105–6] Somewhat similar generalizations-to-be-developed appear in recent Mississippi and Alabama curriculum bulletins, two of which are: "Opportunities for exploitation increase as interdependence grows." [223:52] "The few tend to control the means of production." [56:22] In addition, the Mississippi course of study states that children should gain an understanding of the possibilities of a higher standard of living due to mass production. [56:250]

Courses published in the industrial Northeast rarely deal with the problem aspects of machine production. In this respect a tentative social studies outline for Manhasset, New York, is an exception; for, among other generalizations-to-be-developed, it states: "Income of the people should be adequate to make the products of industry available to all." [233:31] Manhasset, it should be said, is not an industrial but a residential community.

7. AWARENESS OF THE STRUGGLE FOR ECONOMIC DEMOCRACY

In reading elementary courses of study one cannot escape the conclusion that American children practically everywhere are being taught that democracy was achieved long ago. Only now and then does one find a course that mentions even indirectly the twentieth-century struggle to control the American economy in the interests of all the people. The struggle is suggested in some of the excerpts quoted above regarding the possibilities inherent in machine production. The following are the only other indications found in statements of philosophy and aims that course of study writers expect the struggle for economic democracy to be recognized in the elementary school.

In the Colorado course for elementary schools a central objective is:

An understanding of the relation of the progress of democracy to (1) earning a living and the production of goods and services, and (2) to the distribution and use of goods and services. [41:4]

One objective of *A Suggested Unit on Co-operation* for Minnesota schools is:

"To teach the relationship between democracy in political life and in economic life." [235:Pt. I, 3]

In the St. Louis County program in social studies an objective is:

"Appreciation of and desire to realize the American dream of equal opportunity for all." [183:23]

Understandings sought by the Virginia course of study include:

(1) A privileged minority having wealth derived from business and industry has succeeded the landed aristocracy; (2) Some forces in modern business resist government regulation in behalf of all the people; (3) The methods of distribution of goods tend to direct social products into the hands of the few. [73:10–1]

"Knowledge of the tendency of privileged classes to exploit weaker groups" is a desired outcome of a fifth grade unit used in Fort Worth. [132:29] In the same grade is to be developed the generalization that "The first-comers into a country have a better opportunity for economic, social, and political influence than those who come later." [132:59]

An understanding to be sought in "The Story of Commerce," a Missouri unit for sixth grade, is:

The happiness and success of a people depend very much upon its system of distributing the products of its fields and factories among its population. [57:944]

"How our government is trying to improve our methods of production and distribution so that all may have a fair share in the products of our physical environment" is an understanding sought in the Houston course in social studies for sixth grade. [154:2]

In Manhasset, New York, a generalization-to-be-developed in grades five and six is:

"A more equitable distribution of the products of man's labor is needed." [233:15]

It is evident that in their statements of philosophy or aims only a very small proportion of elementary courses of study touch upon the struggle for economic democracy.

8. AWARENESS OF THE ADAPTATIONS DEMANDED BY AN INCREASINGLY INTERDEPENDENT ECONOMY

During the past decade the interdependence theme has been incorporated into most elementary courses of study. The attention of children is directed to the interdependence of: (1) the members of the family, (2) the family and the community, (3) the city workers and the farmers, (4) the various regions of the United States, and (5) the various countries. The practical consequences of interdependence, as brought out in those few courses of study which in their statements of philosophy and aims make any of the consequences explicit, appear to be: (1) the need to create a more cooperative and less individualistic society; (2) the need for greater economic cooperation between nations; (3) the responsibility of the community for providing the basic necessaries of life when the individual is unable to provide them for himself; (4) the need to support and use the increasing variety of community and government services. Illustrative statements for each of these four consequences are given below.

(a) *The need to create a more cooperative and less individualistic society*. According to the Denver kindergarten-primary program in social studies:

> The school must contribute to constructing a co-operative society by providing experiences which: (*a*) help the child see the part co-operation is playing in his school, home, and community relationships; (*b*) encourage a growing sense of responsibility for co-operating in all these groups; (*c*) cause the child to think about and question certain shortages in human society which are due to a lack of co-operation; (*d*) help the child to vision and work increasingly for an improved world society in which the co-operative nature of human activities will result in a happy, satisfying life. [127:14]

The authors of a recent Louisiana curriculum bulletin write:

> The democratic philosophy of education recognizes the importance and worth of every individual and insists that schools and life outside the school, working together, must so educate every child that his activities finally shall be directed toward co-operative group service rather than individual aggrandizement and that his success in life shall be measured by his worth to society rather than by accumulated material wealth gotten through non-social practices. [231:39–40]

The Virginia course of study seeks the understanding that:

> Inventions and discoveries increase the need for co-operative living and co-operative thinking. [73:145]

"Individualism will not meet the needs of co-operative living" is a generalization-to-be-developed in Alabama schools. [223:54]

The opposite of individualism is concern for the common good, to develop which is an objective (expressed or implied) of all public schools. Thus, a recent Michigan bulletin suggests that the teacher evaluate her work by asking herself: "Do I encourage my pupils to desire the promotion of the common good rather than the selfish advancement of the individual?" [54:20] To the extent that children do develop a concern for the common good it is obvious that they will be prepared to function in a more cooperative economy than we have at the present time. What proportion of course of study writers would regard such an economy as desirable, it is impossible to say.

(b) *The need for greater economic cooperation between nations.* That nations are becoming more interdependent, both culturally and economically, is a commonplace generalization in elementary curriculum bulletins; but mention of any of the economic consequences thereof was found in the objectives of only three courses of study.

The Missouri course of study for sixth grade aims to develop the understanding that:

The success of a nation in a world growing more and more interdependent, depends upon its resources and industries being effectively used in a scheme of international trade. [57:944]

Houston fifth graders are to learn that:

There are many causes of war. One element that tends to promote misunderstanding and strife is selfish economic competition. [151:2]

The Fort Worth social studies course for fifth grade goes farther than any other in the generalization-to-be-developed that:

By wise consumption man must make the wealth of the world go around to all. [132:74]

(c) *The need for the community's assuming responsibility for providing the basic necessaries of life when the individual is unable to provide them for himself.* This concept, which seems to have been generally accepted by the people since 1930, is explicit in extremely few elementary courses of study. Three instances were found.

In a Houston unit for sixth grade occurs the generalization-to-be-developed:

The individual and the community must share the responsibility of providing for the health and safety of all. [156:1]

A Grand Rapids course lists among truths which the small child can gradually understand:

If his parents cannot provide clothing, etc., so that a child can go to school, it should be done by individuals or social agencies. [134:16]

An aim of the State of Washington course in social studies is:

To establish an understanding that the community is mutually responsible for the establishment and maintenance of a proper place to live. [193:4]

(d) *The need to support and use the increasing variety of community and government services.* This consequence of interdependence is an implied aim in many elementary bulletins. Sometimes it is explicitly stated, as in the Brockton course in social studies for fifth grade, where one outcome sought is "To develop a desire to make good use of public facilities." [227:3] The Virginia course has as an understanding-to-be-developed:

Citizens improve their status and increase the efficiency of the government when they avail themselves of the wide variety of services of the government. [73:10]

The Saginaw, Michigan, course in social studies seeks the understanding that "People should willingly provide finance for public service." [182:6]

In Allentown, Pennsylvania, where a unit on community services and the community chest is taught annually in every grade, among the objectives are:

To create a desire to have a share in the work that is being done by the community service agencies. . . . To help boys and girls to see the significance of each social service resource. [224:n. p.]

9. Understanding of the Importance of Conserving Human and Material Resources, Including Natural Beauty

To teach the importance of conserving property and natural resources is an objective of a great many elementary courses of study. That human beings are an economic resource, and that they can be conserved, is a concept that is only beginning to gain recognition in the elementary curriculum.

The following excerpts illustrate the occurrence of the conservation objective:

To acquire an appreciation of the value of the natural resources of the state; to acquire an appreciation of the importance of state and national thrift through the wise use of natural resources.[1]

To gain an understanding of the proper use of land and natural resources.[2]

To lead the pupils to an appreciation of the beauty of nature as an economic asset.[3]

---

[1] Detroit, Michigan, *Course of Study in Elementary Social Science*, p. 88. 1932.

[2] Oklahoma City, *Revised Course of Study: Social Science, Grades IV–VI*, p. 1. 1936.

[3] Minnesota, *Curriculum for Elementary Schools*, p. 495. 1928.

World conservation of all natural resources is essential to prosperity.[4]
To appreciate the importance of the conservation of all human and material resources.[5]

Problems that challenge education in Georgia:

The challenge to all schools in Georgia to take account of the varied resources of the state in climate, forests, mines, streams, and people to the end that children may know what Georgia has, and may be able in years to come to develop these resources and preserve for themselves and their children this great natural heritage.[6]

A point of citizenship that should be taught in any well-organized subject; respect for property that belongs to others, especially to the present group and those that will follow. . . . Many children and adults who would not steal from or mar the personal possessions of another individual, friend or stranger, have little conscience about abusing the property of a group because the group seems impersonal. The teaching of attitudes and habits of respect for social property, whether it belongs to school, store, railroad, city, industrial firm, or government is very necessary in our modern organization of life in which so many of the most vital instruments of our civilization are socially rather than individually owned.[7]

10. Thrift and Intelligent Money Management, Including Appreciation of What Parents Have to Spend

Long before it was concerned with any other aspect of economic competence, the public school attempted to inculcate thrift. Emphasis was laid on frugality in the use of school supplies, clothing, and other things that cost money or labor, and on saving money against future need. Then came the time, in the decade following the first World War, when thrift education centered on getting pupils to deposit money weekly in the school savings bank. In the last decade the emphasis has begun to shift from mere saving to intelligent money management, including wise spending. The change is illustrated in a passage from a general course of study entitled *A Study of Curriculum Problems in the North Carolina Public Schools.* After explaining that an act passed in 1933 requires the State to provide in its public schools

---

[4] Fort Worth, *Tentative Course of Study in Social Studies,* p. 74. 1933.
[5] Omaha, Nebraska, *Social Studies, Grades 4–6,* Introduction. 1936.
[6] Georgia, *Guide to Curriculum Improvement,* p. 23. 1937.
[7] North Carolina, *A Study of Curriculum Problems in the North Carolina Public Schools,* p. 280. 1935.

for "instruction in thrift and the principles, practice, and advantage of saving," the writers state:

The terms thrift and saving should not find their only application to money or other material things. They must take on broader meanings. As it relates to the child, thrift would include a proper use of (1) his time, (2) his talent, (3) his energy and effort, (4) his health, both physical and mental, and (5) material things. Hoarding, self-denial and miserliness are not to be construed as characteristic of thrift or of savings. Intelligent spending, based upon personal and social needs and understandings, may be just as much a part of thrift and saving as the saving of money. [63:23]

The newer tendencies in thrift education are suggested by a Texas unit for intermediate grades entitled "Keeping a Personal Budget." It is designed to teach the rudiments of money management by promoting growth in: (1) appreciation of the amount of money parents have to spend; (2) the habit of spending money wisely; (3) willingness to practice thrift; (4) interest in keeping a personal budget; (5) skill in keeping simple accounts and appreciation of their value. The first element in this statement—appreciation of the amount of money parents have to spend—was found in no other bulletin. Its omission seems to indicate a blindness on the part of course of study writers to a common source of tension between children and parents.

11. ABILITY TO MAKE WISE SELECTION AND USE OF GOODS AND SERVICES

This may be more briefly stated as "consumer education." Instruction in the care of foodstuffs, clothing, and the home is often recommended in elementary courses. Instruction in the selection of goods is sometimes recommended.

A Bronxville, New York, curriculum bulletin states that:

Children need to know about and have such experience with materials, processes, and conditions of production as will contribute to their efficiency in selecting, caring for and using products. [228:1]

The following excerpt is from the New Hampshire outline for industrial arts:

Children are daily consumers of the products of industry. In this era of machine-made things, the chief task of the teacher of industrial arts in the elementary school is not to develop skill in the making of articles. Work with material and tools is not primarily for manipulative skill but for understanding and appreciation. The work should help children: (1) to understand and appreciate desirable qualities in material and workmanship, (2) to choose from the multitude of articles on the market those best fitted to meet their needs. . . . (3) to use and care for the products of industry intelligently. . . . [61:161]

Consumer education is necessarily concerned with advertising. Yet learning to evaluate advertising is an expressed objective in very few courses. The strongest declaration in regard to advertising was found in the West Virginia course for elementary grades:

It is very important to teach pupils how to evaluate the numerous kinds and forms of advertising presented today by the press, radio, moving picture, and salesman. It should be a constant aim, as opportunity is presented, to prepare children to resist the advertising of useless, costly, and even harmful commodities. [75:267]

"The ability to judge the merits of claims made by advertisers of articles and services for sale" is a desired outcome of the Virginia program. [73:509] This, it should be said, is the only instance discovered, in statements of philosophy or aims, of consumer attention to the selection of services.

12. An Interest in the Use of Tax Money

The question of how taxes shall be apportioned in meeting community needs is rarely suggested in elementary courses. The best example was found in a Houston social studies unit for sixth grade, one objective of which is:

To become aware of some of the problems confronting Houston citizens, such as: (1) What can be done by the community to improve its parks and other recreational facilities? (2) How can Houston continue to become a better place to live? (3) Should the city continue to improve its shipping facilities? (4) For what purposes should the community levy taxes upon its citizens? . . . [156:2]

13. Knowledge of Productive Processes by Which Individuals, Families, Communities May Increase Their Real Income

For decades many public schools, particularly in rural areas, have given more or less attention to this aim. Approximately half of the general and social studies courses examined suggest that experience be provided in cooking, preserving, sewing, mending, gardening, poultry keeping, or other productive domestic or agricultural processes. Material on gardening, poultry keeping, fruit growing, and the like was also found in a few science courses. An economic motive for including curriculum materials of this sort is specifically avowed in a Salt Lake City bulletin on science, two objectives of which are (1) to reduce the cost of living by gardening, conservation, etc., and (2) to learn ways of supplementing one's income. [220:10–1]

The teaching of productive processes through a vocational course in agriculture is uncommon in the first six grades. However, a Georgia bulletin recommends the study of agriculture in the sixth grade by both boys and girls. [43:322] Without doubt the reason for this recommendation is the belief that through the study of agriculture young people may learn how to get a greater return from farming.

The teaching of ways to increase the real income of the community was not found as an expressed objective. It is an implied objective in occasional suggested activities, as in the problem to discuss: "How can our region attract more sportsmen and tourists?" which occurs in two or three courses. It is implied in the proposal in the Connecticut course in nature study that children try to interest their selectmen in planting a town forest as a source of future revenue. [199:61] This is the most concrete suggestion found for increasing the income of a community.

14. KNOWLEDGE OF COMMON BUSINESS PRACTICES

This objective is often stated in arithmetic courses, though usually not below the sixth grade. For example, a desired outcome from arithmetic, according to the Minnesota course of study, is "an understanding of simple business forms." [55:46] Utah teachers are instructed to:

Introduce near the end of the sixth grade such facts as may be useful in ordinary business activities and as may afford some insight into current business practices and customs involving arithmetic, and to uses of the following business forms and relations: budget, sales slip, promissory note, manufacturing firm, retail company, wholesale company. [111:59]

The importance of teaching the reasons for various business practices is pointed out in the Wyoming course in arithmetic:

Children should be told the reason for the several business practices in order to get a better picture of the process. Children may be able to do interest examples with a reasonable degree of accuracy, but will probably do better work if they know a person pays interest on money for the same reason that he pays money to some one to work for him. The money "works" for him, too. . . . Some children may want to know why the banker pays two per cent for time or savings deposits, yet charges the farmer or rancher six to ten per cent. Or why the rancher receives eight cents a pound for his steer, while John Doe, a shop worker in a town within ten miles of the rancher, must pay thirty cents a pound for portions of the same steer. [114:61]

15. Understanding Some of the Basic Vocabulary of Economics

This objective was found stated in two social studies courses. One of these, a Houston unit for sixth grade, has as an outcome sought:

To know the meaning of exchange, barter, trade, buying and selling, production, distribution, consumption, value or price, and credit as applied to our present day business. [155:2]

The other is a Maryland bulletin on social studies for intermediate grades which asks:

Are the pupils able to use in meaningful content such words as: organize, economic, specialization, industry, production, resource, supply, demand, co-operation, interdependence, utilities, raw materials, market, barter, distribution, capital, labor? [169:141]

SUMMARY

Many elementary courses of study contain no statement of philosophy and aims. Of those that do contain such statements, some mention no objectives related to economic competence, while others mention only such conventional objectives as thrift and the conservation of property. A minority of curriculum bulletins clearly recognize, in statements of philosophy or aims, the need for new kinds of economic education.

All the objectives related to economic competence that were found were classified under fifteen headings (see pp. 34-5). Not one of the curriculum bulletins examined contains all fifteen. The Virginia general program and the Houston program in social studies each contain about two-thirds of these objectives, while the Alabama curriculum bulletins, the Mississippi general program, and the Fort Worth program in social studies each contain about one-half. Various bulletins contain three, four, or five of the fifteen objectives.

The economic objectives most commonly stated are, in descending order of their frequency:

1. The practice of thrift.
2. The conservation of material resources and property.
3. A knowledge of common business terms and practice.
4. Occupational orientation.
5. Ability to select and use consumer goods.
6. Understanding of social-economic problems.

Although the term "interdependence" occurs in nearly all lists of understandings- and generalizations-to-be-developed, the economic consequences of interdependence and the adaptations it requires are seldom suggested.

Similarly, many lists of understandings- and generalizations-to-be-developed contain some reference to the fact that we live in the machine age, but few definitely indicate that it is important to understand the problems that the machine has brought us, or the possibilities for good and evil that inhere in mass production.

Of the economic objectives found, the following were least common:

1. Evaluation of advertising.
2. Ability to select and use consumer services.
3. Knowledge of productive processes by which individuals, families, and communities may increase their real incomes.
4. An interest in the use of tax money.
5. Conservation of natural beauty.
6. Intelligent money management other than the practice of thrift.
7. Appreciation of what parents have to spend.
8. An interest in the democratic planning of social-economic change.
9. Awareness that the community is responsible for providing the basic necessaries of life when the individual cannot provide them for himself.
10. Understandings related to the struggle to achieve economic democracy.
11. Development of the basic vocabulary of economics.

A few of the objectives least commonly found in statements of philosophy or aims are implied fairly often in the content of courses of study. Among these are items 3, 4, 5, and 6 above.

The fact that an objective is expressed does not necessarily mean, of course, that it will influence the content of the program outlined. In some bulletins there appears to have been no attempt to provide materials which might help to produce the desired outcomes. Evidence of the real objectives, as distinguished from objectives that are merely stated, may be found in the suggested activities and the problems proposed for study. Chapter Four presents materials selected from all the courses in the four samples which may furnish clues to the real objectives having to do with economic competence, both in bulletins which contain statements of philosophy or aims and in those which do not.

Topics in General and Social Studies Courses and Their Contribution to Education for Economic Competence

THE present chapter is concerned with the following three problems:

1. What commonly occurring topics and activities in general and social studies courses for the first six grades are likely to be the vehicles for learnings having a significant relation to economic competence?

2. In how many courses and on what grade levels does each topic or activity appear at least once?

3. What course of study materials related to the topics listed are likely to contribute to economic competence?

FIFTY-SIX TOPICS SIGNIFICANT FOR ECONOMIC COMPETENCE

The methods used in selecting topics have been given in detail on pp. 27–8 and will be summarized here.

A tentative list of eighty topics and activities around which the learnings related to economic competence appear to cluster was drawn up. As counting proceeded, some topics were dropped because they were not well defined, because their economic implications were practically never brought out, or because they occurred only in the arithmetic outlines of general courses. After the analysis was completed the topics which had been found in courses from fewer than three places were listed separately (see Table VIII, p. 146). Fifty-six topics were left, and these were classified in seven groups, arranged in descending order of importance according to the average frequency of each group. The topics within each group were arranged in the same manner. The seven groups are given below.

GROUP I. INDUSTRIES AND OCCUPATIONS IN THE MODERN WORLD

1. Farming, gardening, stock-raising
2. Transportation
3. Manufacturing
4. Communication
5. Mining and quarrying
6. Lumbering, forestry, forest products
7. Fishing
8. Store-keeping
9. Recreation industry; travel for recreation
10. Local occupations in general
11. Construction workers and industry
12. Electric power industry

Each topic in Group I appears on the average in 38 per cent of the 420 general and social studies courses tabulated.

GROUP II. HOME LIFE IN OUR COMMUNITY

13. Diet: selecting a healthful
14. House: planning and constructing
15. Clothing: selection of
16. Sewing, mending, or dyeing
17. House: caring for and improving
18. House: furnishing and decorating
19. Food: actual preparation or preservation
20. Clothing: care of
21. Textiles: kinds, selection of
22. Refreshments: actual serving to guests
23. Toys: care, repair, making, selection of
24. Remedies and treatments: selection of
25. Household preparations

Each topic in Group II appears on the average in 30 per cent of the 420 general and social studies courses tabulated.

GROUP III. CONSERVATION

26. Forests, flowers, and wild life
27. Water control

28. Soils and minerals

Each topic in Group III appears on the average in 28 per cent of the 420 general and social studies courses tabulated.

GROUP IV.   LOCAL COMMUNITY SERVICES AND THEIR SUPPORT

29. Recreational facilities
30. Fire and police protection
31. Health protection
32. Water supply; sewage disposal
33. Public school system
34. Taxation

Each topic in Group IV appears on the average in 20 per cent of the 420 general and social studies courses tabulated.

GROUP V.   CHARACTERISTICS OF A MACHINE CIVILIZATION

35. Interdependence
36. Trade; markets
37. World trade; tariffs
38. Machines: how they have changed our ways of living
39. Standards of living: comparative
40. Labor conditions and problems
41. Mass production; specialization
42. Unemployment
43. Growth of big business; regulation of business
44. Labor organization; strikes; lockouts
45. Distribution of income; concentration of wealth
46. Prospects of attaining an adequate standard of living

Each topic in Group V occurs on the average in 15 per cent of the 420 general and social studies courses tabulated.

GROUP VI.   MONEY MANAGEMENT

47. Budgets
48. Cash accounts
49. Giving to worthy causes
50. Thrift in buying
51. Advertising: caution in responding to
52. Consumer credit: how to use

Each topic in Group VI occurs on the average in 7 per cent of the 420 general and social studies courses tabulated.

GROUP VII. BUSINESS ORGANIZATION; BANKING

53. Banks: varied services of
54. Cooperatives
55. Government ownership
56. Organization of private enterprise

Each topic in Group VII occurs on the average in 4 per cent of the 420 general and social studies courses tabulated.

The median topic of the entire list of fifty-six appears in 19.5 per cent of the general and social studies courses tabulated.

THE FREQUENCY TABLES AND THEIR SIGNIFICANCE

The number of courses in which each topic appears, and their grade levels, are given in Tables I to VII. Each table contains one of the seven groups of topics listed above, and bears a corresponding number.

The methods used in tabulating the results were described in detail in Chapter II (pp. 29–30). It should be recalled that a topic was checked but once for each course, and that it was counted even though it appeared only in a list of suggested activities, and even though it was represented merely by one of its sub-topics. Accordingly, the figures given in Tables I to VII refer to the number of courses in which each topic appears *once or oftener*.

It should not be supposed that each topic is so treated in every course in which it appears that its implications for economic competence are brought out. The topics in Table I (Industries and Occupations in the Modern World), in Table IV (Local Community Services and Their Support), and in Table V (Characteristics of a Machine Civilization) are often presented in courses of study without, apparently, any consideration of how they might contribute to economic competence. On the other hand, most of the topics in Table II (Home Life in Our Community), Table III (Conservation), Table VI (Money Management), and Table VII (Business Organization and Banking) are so obviously related to economic competence that they may be assumed to carry some of the information and to suggest some of the understandings contributory to that goal whenever they are included.

The topics may be regarded as the framework on which the learnings necessary to economic competence are most likely to be developed, assuming that the course of study writer or the classroom teacher is interested in developing these learnings.

THE MATERIALS SELECTED TO ILLUSTRATE ECONOMIC CONTENT

Materials were collected from courses to illustrate how each of the fifty-six topics may carry learnings that are likely to contribute to economic competence. The materials do not embrace all the economic learnings which might be related to a given topic, but only those found in the courses read.

So far as possible, the materials finally selected were taken from courses included in the four samples (see p. 27). Occasionally, material has been included from a course outside the samples; such material may be recognized because its source is marked "not tabulated."

Much of the material has been taken from social studies courses. Much also comes from general courses, and usually, but not always, from the social studies section of these courses. Some of the material comes from separate arithmetic and science courses, and is included because it brings out economic learnings not covered in the social studies and general courses which were examined. The source of each item is given in abbreviated form, the complete title being found in the final Bibliography (pp. 174–87). It should be noted that many of the items are not exact quotations, but have been condensed by omitting unnecessary or irrelevant details.

A considerable number of the activities and problems collected occur but once or twice in all the courses examined. Therefore, it must not be supposed that materials similar to those presented in the following pages are likely to be found in any recently published course taken at random. However, every modern social studies course will contain the equivalent of some of these materials, and a few complete elementary programs, in which unusual attention is given to education for economic competence, will contain the equivalent of one-third to one-half of them.

These materials are not intended to be used as a course of study. Some of the problems and activities may not be suitable for city children; others may not meet the needs of rural children. Some appear on a lower grade level than may prove most desirable for their initial presentation to children of average ability. It is not the purpose of this investigation to recommend materials or to indicate on what grade levels the various learnings should begin. Its purpose is to draw attention to the wide variety of economic materials now included in courses for the first six grades.

The remainder of this chapter is divided into eight parts, the first seven dealing with the seven major groups of topics, and the eighth with a supplementary list of topics occurring in courses from fewer than three places.

GROUP I. INDUSTRIES AND OCCUPATIONS IN THE MODERN WORLD

Each of the twelve topics in this group appears on the average in 159 courses (38 per cent) of the 420 general and social studies courses tabulated. The average for the next most frequent group is 124. The numerical preponderance of Group I indicates that it is the most important channel for economic learnings in the elementary school.

To what extent may the study of these topics contribute to education for economic competence? Without attempting to say how much should be achieved on the elementary level, the investigator believes that the study of industries and occupations in the modern world may be expected to increase a person's economic competence by—

1. Giving him an acquaintance with productive processes which may improve his ability to select and use the products.

2. Giving him an acquaintance with merchandising, transportation, communication, and recreational services which may improve his ability to select and use these services.

3. Giving him a wider and more informed choice of occupations.

4. Informing him regarding occupations that are more crowded or more hazardous than the average.

5. Acquainting him with the way businesses of various types are organized and managed.

6. Increasing his understanding of the problems involved in the principal industries, and particularly farming.

7. Making clear the dependence of any enterprise upon adequate supplies of raw materials, labor, managerial skill, and capital.

8. Creating a realization of the importance of conserving natural resources.

9. Giving him some insight into the way prices of products or services are determined.

Evidence in the present study of how much, if at all, the elementary school attempts to achieve these objectives consists of the following:

1. An analysis of the declared objectives of elementary courses of study. (See Chapter Three)

2. A table showing the number of general and social studies courses in which each topic in this group appears. (See Table I)

3. Samples of course of study materials selected to indicate the range of activities and problems likely to contribute to economic competence connected with each topic in this group (see pp. 62–78).

4. Tables showing the number of courses in which certain related topics appear. See especially Table V, Characteristics of a Machine Civilization (p. 114); Table VII, Business Organization; Banking (p. 141); and Table IX, Topics Bearing on Economic Competence Found in Arithmetic Courses (p. 150–1).

COUNTING THE TWELVE TOPICS IN GROUP I

The first problem was to determine which industries and occupations are treated in elementary courses and in how many courses they are treated. It was arbitrarily decided that occupations in the medical profession should be counted under "Health protection," of firemen and policemen, under "Fire and Police protection," of teachers and other workers in schools, under "Public School System," of persons engaged in distribution other than store-keepers, under "Trade" or "World Trade," of bankers, under "Banking," and of conservation workers (i.e., forest rangers, game wardens, etc.), under the group of conservation topics. With these exceptions it was found that the industries dealt with in elementary courses can be readily classified under the twelve topics given in Table I.

A passing reference to an industry was not counted, as, for example,

TABLE I

INDUSTRIES AND OCCUPATIONS IN THE MODERN WORLD

Topics Related to Economic Competence Found in General and Social Studies Courses

NUMBER AND PER CENT OF COURSES IN WHICH TOPIC APPEARS*

TOPIC	COMBINED COURSES (420)		GENERAL COURSES (210)								SOCIAL STUDIES COURSES (210)							
	No.	%	1	2	3	4	5	6	Total	%	1	2	3	4	5	6	Total	%
			Grades								Grades							
1. Farming, gardening, stock-raising	314	75	23	21	21	26	28	25	144	69	27	24	26	31	33	29	170	81
2. Transportation	257	61	11	23	20	19	29	24	126	60	16	19	26	19	26	25	131	62
3. Manufacturing	232	55	5	11	18	21	28	25	108	51	6	16	20	23	30	29	124	59
4. Communication	212	51	11	20	15	16	22	17	101	48	20	22	16	17	21	21	111	53
5. Mining and quarrying	159	38	0	4	9	16	25	21	75	36	1	2	10	17	27	27	84	40
6. Lumbering, forestry, forest products	147	35	0	3	6	19	21	17	66	31	0	2	9	17	29	24	81	39
7. Fishing	132	31	0	3	4	12	18	13	50	24	0	4	7	27	26	18	82	39
8. Store-keeping	121	29	19	23	8	4	3	2	59	28	23	23	9	5	0	2	62	30
9. Recreation industry; travel for recreation	97	23	1	1	3	9	15	15	44	21	1	1	5	13	23	10	53	25
10. Local occupations in general	91	22	11	13	8	7	3	3	45	21	15	11	9	5	1	5	46	22
11. Construction workers and industry	80	19	8	6	5	6	5	6	36	17	11	9	10	6	7	1	44	21
12. Electric power industry	63	15	0	1	1	1	10	11	24	11	0	1	3	13	8	14	39	17

* A course is the program for a single grade. For each grade 35 general courses and 35 social studies courses were tabulated.

in the statement that "The Norwegians live by fishing, shipping, farming, and lumbering." An industry was counted only if taken up in some detail.

In the case of the topic "Local occupations in general," a merely passing reference to a variety of local occupations or a detailed study of two or three local occupations was not counted. Inclusion of this topic depended on some indication that many of the occupations in the community were to be considered, as, for example, in such statements as: "Discuss how the people of this community earn a living" and "Have pupils tell about the work their fathers do."

MATERIALS FROM COURSES OF STUDY ILLUSTRATING THE CONTENT OF TOPICS IN GROUP I LIKELY TO CONTRIBUTE TO ECONOMIC COMPETENCE

In reading this chapter, the meaning of certain abbreviated forms must be kept in mind. The numbers in the line which follows the descriptive title of each topic are percentages, to be read as explained in the footnote on this page. In the citations following the items, the abbreviation "Soc. Stu." refers to a social studies bulletin, and "g." means grade. To learn the exact title of the bulletin from which an item is taken, it is necessary to turn in the Bibliography to the list of social studies, general, arithmetic, or science bulletins, as the case may be, and to locate the cited course by author—the author being the board of education in the place named in the citation.

Topic 1. The Farming Industry. Gardening, dairying, stock-raising, farm problems, government aid to farmers.
General: primary 62%, intermediate 75%. Social Studies: primary 73%, intermediate 89%.*

This extremely common topic is developed in a variety of ways. Often the materials are purely descriptive. In their emphasis on improved methods, costs, earnings, or farm problems, the following samples are superior to the average.

Agriculture is sometimes found as a separate subject for rural schools

---

* This line is to be read as follows: This topic was found in 62 per cent of 105 general courses for primary grades; it was found in 75 per cent of 105 general courses for intermediate grades. It was found in 73 per cent of 105 social studies courses for primary grades and it was found in 89 per cent of 105 social studies courses for intermediate grades.

as low as the sixth grade, but the materials below were selected from social studies, science, and general courses rather than from courses in agriculture.

MATERIALS AIMED AT IMPROVING FARMING METHODS

Essential learnings: how to candle eggs, set a hen, build a coop, make a garden, test seed corn. [Missouri, Soc. Stu., g. 2, pp. 869–74]

Finding out about different kinds of chickens. Which are best for eggs and which for meat? Finding out how chickens are raised. Visiting a poultry ranch if feasible. Discussing brooding. Hatching some chickens. Keeping chickens in the school yard and caring for them. Finding out about various ways in which eggs are used. [Los Angeles County, Soc. Stu., g. 5, p. 59]

Learn the names of common weeds, the ways weeds harm other plants, ways to get rid of weeds. [Iowa, Science, g. 4–6 p. 96]

Collect garden information. Grow plants inside, prepare the garden, make cold frames, make spray mixtures, spray or dust plants, cultivate the garden, transplant, harvest, can garden products. What local conditions should one investigate before becoming a market gardener? [Massachusetts, Science, g. 6, pp. 95–6]

Why are forage plants important to the farmer? Find out the best methods of growing and harvesting the common forage crops. Discuss the value of some of the forage crops. [Binghamton, Soc. Stu., g. 6, *How Agriculture Supplies Our Needs and Wants*, p. 14]

Visit a demonstration farm or some up-to-date farm. Study the control of the more common plant and animal diseases occurring in the community. Observe the use of crankcase oil to prevent rust of farm machinery. Observe the effects of weathering on painted and unpainted wood and tools. Committees may study intensively such topics as crop rotation, use of fertilizer, the electric farm, etc. [Texas, General, g. 6, pp. 84–6]

Make a booklet of the farm pupils would like to own. Draw farm to scale with number of acres of various crops. Include pictures of farm homes, barns, machinery, animals, and modern home conveniences. Plan the proper rotation and diversification of crops to improve the soil. Report on what should be done to prevent dust storms, and on the value of farm woodlots. Is there any land in your township not now under cultivation that it would pay to cultivate? [Kansas, Soc. Stu., g. 6, pp. 304–5]

Note: the items above do not show the entire range of activities and problems pertaining to agricultural methods. Materials on cotton farming, fruit growing, sheep raising, and other types of agriculture were also found in the courses tabulated.

THE FARMER'S COSTS AND EARNINGS

Discuss the capital invested in a dairy farm, and the value of farm, stock, buildings, and implements. Discuss the overhead expenses of the dairy farmer for help, bottles, delivery truck, etc. [New York,[1] Arithmetic, g. 4, pp. 71–2]

Determine approximately the grain farmer's profit, considering current prices of seed grains, amount of seed grain required per acre, cost of labor, and current selling price of grain. Write original problems to find cost of marketing, cost of machinery to raise crops, etc. [Binghamton, Soc. Stu., g. 6, *How Agriculture Supplies Our Needs and Wants,* pp. 12–3]

Raising apples, potatoes, wheat, cost of selling, packing, etc.; profits, losses. [Idaho, Arithmetic, g. 6, p. 63]

Computing the savings to the family through raising their own vegetables. [Illinois, Arithmetic, g. 4–6, p. 30]

Computing saving from keeping poultry. [Sacramento, Arithmetic, g. 5, p. 49]

ECONOMIC IMPORTANCE OF DAIRYING

Investigating the economic importance of the dairy industry in Mississippi; amount and retail value of milk used in pupils' homes, the community, and the state; number of milch cows and number of men employed in dairying. [Mississippi, General, g. 6, p. 255]

THE MARKETING OF FARM PRODUCTS

Why are commission merchants necessary in our modern community life? Why does the farmer not find it always to his advantage to sell directly to the consumer at a higher price than he can get from the commission merchant? [Houston, high g. 6, unit 3, p. 56]

Investigate the difference in price paid to the farmer for milk and that paid by the consumer. Discuss its justification. [Mississippi, General, g. 6, p. 255]

Treat very simply and concretely: the low prices for farm products, the milk strike, marketing problems, especially roadside marketing. [Madison, Soc. Stu., g. 5, p. 26]

FARM PROBLEMS; GOVERNMENT AID TO FARMERS[2]

How does it happen that most of the farmers of the world are poor men, while the manufacturers are rich men? [Detroit, Soc. Stu., g. 6, p. 256]

[1] Throughout this chapter "New York" refers to the state and not the city.

[2] Consideration of the agricultural problem was definitely indicated in ten of the general courses and in twelve of the social studies courses tabulated.

In what sections have geographic conditions forced the farmers to turn to other work to supplement their incomes? [Binghamton, Soc. Stu., g. 6, *How Agriculture Supplies Our Needs and Wants*, p. 28]

Why has agriculture in New England changed? (Competition of agricultural regions elsewhere, relief, soils, etc.) (p. 55) Why is the South gradually turning to mixed farming? (p. 59) [Ithaca, Soc. Stu., g. 5]

What is the future of people engaged in agriculture? How can they obtain new lands? Should government authority be used as a measure of control over supply and demand? What probable inventions and improvements may influence farming? Discuss increasing tenancy. Map and compare agricultural areas in the United States which have high and low economic value. [Missouri, General, g. 4, pp. 905–6]

Joan brought an article from the paper on the government's restriction of cotton acreage. The question arose, "How will this affect prices?" Committees were chosen to watch quotations to see the effect of this control. Graphs were made to show the changes in the quotations. [Minneapolis, Arithmetic, g. 6, p. 99]

Why has the western farmer recently substituted the use of horses for the use of gasoline to draw his farm machines? [Baltimore, Science, g. 6, p. 206]

Find out about government services to farmers: weather information and warnings, assistance in emergencies, drought, and flood, help in fighting disease and insect pests, agricultural colleges, boys' and girls' clubs, bulletins. [Madison, Soc. Stu., g. 5, p. 26]

Gather information about how the government helps the Minnesota farmers, how much it spends to kill grasshoppers, etc. [Minneapolis, Arithmetic, g. 5, p. 65]

Topic 2. The Transportation Industry.
General: primary 51%; intermediate 69%. Social Studies: primary 58%; intermediate 67%.

Although this topic appears in most elementary bulletins, often being repeated in several grades, not much of the material bears on the economic aspects of transportation.

IMPORTANCE OF RAPID TRANSPORTATION

Make trips to see automobiles, trains, airplanes, boats, etc. Discuss how the city depends on means of transportation. Discuss how the farmer depends on transportation for the marketing of his products. [Indiana, Soc. Stu., g. 2, p. 47]

How has the coming of railroads and good roads changed the industries and character of the farming in your community? [Connecticut, Science, ungraded, p. 93]

How are the occupations of the people in our community affected by transportation? How have modern methods of transportation affected our homes, food, clothes, and leisure? Why are the types of transportation constantly changing? [Delaware, Soc. Stu., g. 3, p. 73]

Find out what improvements the city of Houston has made in order to facilitate its trade by water; by rail; by overland truck service; by air service. [Houston, high g. 6, unit 1, p. 38]

TRANSPORTATION COSTS; RAILROADING

Is travel by land or sea more expensive? Why are freight rates by water cheaper than overland rates? [Amarillo, Science, g. 5, p. 3]

Study relative costs of various modes of transportation. [San Antonio, Arithmetic, g. 6, p. 128]

Pupils' interests may lead to finding the number of miles per gallon of gas obtained at various rates of speed; finding the cost of running a car including gas, oil, and repairs; discussing automobile inspection regulations. [Mississippi, General, pp. 386-7, grade not specified]

What kinds of passenger trains are there? Railroad cars? Who are some of the workers on a train, in the depot, and in the roundhouse, and what do they do? Who gets the money we pay for tickets and for goods transported? Could we get along without trains? (The railroads pay taxes to the cities, towns, and counties through which they pass; they furnish work to many people; they give transportation service.) [Iowa, History, g. 1-2, p. 19]

Computing wages of men on train crews. [Sacramento, Arithmetic, g. 5, p. 50]

How may one become part owner of a railroad? [Houston, Soc. Stu., low g. 6, unit 1, p. 39]

Visiting the Long Beach airport. Building concepts of cost of fuel used in operating aircraft; of salaries paid employees; of fares to various points. [Long Beach, Arithmetic, g. 6, p. 30]

Discuss means of securing lower transportation rates for Texas fruit growers. (High transportation rates make it impossible for Texas citrus fruits to compete successfully with those of California. California can place a carload of fruit on the New York market for less than Texas can.) [Fort Worth, Soc. Stu., g. 3, p. 166]

For what types of traffic is the railroad best suited? What are some of the large problems of a great railroad company? How do these problems differ from those of other companies operating great transportation networks? What is the future of river transportation? [Missouri, General, g. 5, p. 925]

IMPORTANCE OF GOOD ROADS

Of what are roads made? Which are most expensive to build? To use? Why? Why are good roads important? [Washington,[3] General, g. 6, p. 391]

What kinds of roads does our community now have? Why does our community, state, and nation need to develop land transportation? What kinds of construction materials should we use? Consider cost, durability, utility of local labor, accessibility, etc. [Missouri, General, g. 5, p. 924]

Discuss whether the fine roads in Switzerland are a good investment at their tremendous cost of construction. (g. 4, p. 132) Find out how Texas gets money for her highways. (g. 5, p. 115) [Fort Worth, Soc. Stu.]

Topic 3. The Manufacturing Industry.
General: primary 32%; intermediate 70%. Social Studies: primary 40%; intermediate 78%.

On the primary level this topic is usually limited to a consideration of the processing or manufacturing of food products, such as milk, butter, and bread. On the intermediate level it usually deals with the characteristics of a manufacturing region; occasionally it touches the effects of industrialization; rarely it indicates some of the consumer interests in manufactures.

STUDY OF A SINGLE INDUSTRY

Visiting a grist mill to see how corn and wheat are made into meal and flour. [Arkansas, General, g. 1–3, p. 93]

Our Shoe Industry. Objectives: To learn how shoes are made, the kinds of shoes, how leather is tanned, how to care for shoes, the centers of the shoe industry. [Brockton, Soc. Stu., g. 3, p. 21]

STUDY OF MANUFACTURING IN THE LOCAL COMMUNITY

Find out what manufactured articles are made in Binghamton; discuss reasons for the making of these particular products here. [Binghamton, Soc. Stu., g. 6, *How Manufacturing Supplies Our Needs and Wants,* p. 21]

[3] Throughout this chapter "Washington" refers to the state and not the city.

CHARACTERISTICS OF A MANUFACTURING REGION

Discuss: Influences that have made the United States the chief manufacturing country of the world; raw materials used in the manufacturing centers and their sources; importance of water power for manufacturing; relation between manufacturing and the iron and steel industry. [Denver, Soc. Stu., g. 6, pp. 131–4]

Read to find why northeastern United States should have become one of the chief manufacturing regions of the world; similarly for northwestern Europe. Read to find what countries are beginning to develop more manufacturing. Discuss the reasons. [Binghamton, *op. cit.*, pp. 21–6]

HOW MANUFACTURING AFFECTS LIVING CONDITIONS AND POPULATION

Discuss the relation between high standards of living and the development of manufacturing in the United States. [Denver, Soc. Stu., g. 6, p. 132]

Discuss the ways of living in a typical modern manufacturing region and compare with those in an agricultural region. List the desirable leisure-time activities for home workers and for factory workers. Discuss how the development of manufacturing has affected the population of any industrial section of the United States. [Binghamton, *op. cit.*, pp. 21–6]

CONSUMER INTERESTS IN MANUFACTURES

Find and bring to class examples of manufactured articles which have recently been improved to appeal to the consumer. Discuss the present trend of beautifying the designs of manufactured products; the effects upon sales, and the change it brings to the home and community. Discuss the differences between any article made by hand and the same article made by machinery. [Binghamton, *op. cit.*, pp. 22–3]

Topic 4. The Communication Industry; Using Communication Facilities.

General: primary 44%; intermediate 52%. Social Studies: primary 55%; intermediate 50%.

In grades one and two this topic usually indicates a trip to the post office, playing games in the classroom suggested by activities at the post office, and discussing duties of postal clerks and postmen and the way to address and mail letters and packages. In the intermediate grades communication by telephone, telegraph, cable, radio, and newspaper is usually indicated. The history of communication receives most emphasis, but in some courses attention is also given to the costs and suitability of the several methods of communication, and to the effect of modern devices of communication upon business and the standard of living.

THE POSTAL SYSTEM

What happens to a letter we send by ordinary mail? By special delivery? By air mail? Discuss the right way to mail packages and letters. Discuss the duties of the people who work in a post office. Discuss how postal employees are paid. [Iowa, History, g. 1–2, pp. 20–1]

Visit a post office to observe the work done there. Discuss the different modes of transporting mail. Collect postage stamps to study the different kinds issued by the Post Office Department. Find out what happens to a letter from the time it is mailed until it reaches its destination. [Mississippi, General, g. 2, pp. 129–32]

Finding out how much mail carriers are paid each month and who pays them. Finding out what is done with letters having incomplete or illegible addresses. Finding out why mail service is so important to the rural community. [South Dakota, Soc. Stu., g. 2, pp. 129–30]

Discuss the advantages of postal money orders. Why do we register some mail? Find out the cost of sending parcel post packages, letters, air mail, registered mail, etc. Learn about work in the post office, government employees, and Civil Service. Collect and fill out the various forms used in a post office. [San Mateo County, Soc. Stu., g. 5, pp. 136–9]

Determine the size of the United States postal system today. Compare its expenses and revenue. How are positions in the postal service obtained? [Fort Worth, Arithmetic, g. 6, p. 231]

OTHER METHODS OF COMMUNICATION

Discussing the need of telephones on farms. Finding out how telephone systems are put into rural communities. Finding out how telegrams may be sent from rural homes. [South Dakota, Soc. Stu., g. 2, p. 129]

How does the telegraph save in money and time? How state a telegraph message, compute the cost, and send it? Answer want ads for a position. [San Mateo County, Soc. Stu., g. 5, pp. 136–9]

Finding the cost of sending messages by telegraph, telephone, and cable. Comparing with the cost of sending messages in colonial days. [Houston, Soc. Stu., low g. 6, unit 2, p. 29]

Assume that you are a stockbroker and list the numerous communication devices you would have in your office. Write a class play in which the telephone, telegraph, cable, postal service, newspaper, wireless, and radio are personified, and debate their usefulness to man. [Fort Worth, Soc. Stu., g. 6, p. 36]

Find out who pays for radio broadcasts and the average cost per minute of broadcasting. Estimate the cost of broadcasting a fifteen-minute program. (g. 4, p. 120) Discuss why some hours of the day are more popular for listening to the radio and hence more expensive to broadcasters. Investigate and report on the various positions connected with radio work that might be chosen as a vocation. Find out the length and cost of the preparation period, the advantages of such work, the working hours, and the possible remuneration. (g. 6, p. 228) Estimate the amount of capital necessary to conduct a large newspaper for one year. Compare with the amount required to publish a paper seventy-five years ago. (g. 4, p. 120) [Fort Worth, Arithmetic]

In keeping accounts for their school paper the children found that the price of two cents a copy hardly more than covered the cost. They asked how the newspapers published in the city could be sold for three cents. A committee went to each newspaper to learn the price for advertising per inch, column, and page. We estimated the amount of advertising in the weekday and the Sunday edition. We saw that our newspapers are supported by their advertisers and may therefore be influenced by them. [Springfield, Arithmetic, g. 6, p. 30]

EFFECTS OF RAPID COMMUNICATION UPON SOCIETY

How does communication affect our standards of living? Our economic interdependence? How has communication made the world small with respect to distance and in terms of time? Determine how communication has affected specialization of activities. Find out how communication and transportation are dependent one upon the other. Watch the current event articles for improvements in the various devices for communication. [Missouri, Soc. Stu., g. 6, pp. 941–3]

Topic 5. Mining; Quarrying.
General: primary 12%; intermediate 59%. Social Studies; primary 12%; intermediate 68%.

This topic occurs most often in geography outlines for the fifth and sixth grades. The materials are usually purely descriptive. The conservation aspects are seldom indicated. (See topic 28, pp. 103–4)

What minerals and stones can be found within your town? What businesses have been developed from the minerals and stones taken from the ground in your community? [Connecticut, Science, ungraded, pp. 92–3]

What kinds of mines has Colorado? What kinds of mines are near your community? How do we use the minerals taken from mines? Where are minerals made into things we use? What other communities are dependent on our community for minerals? How is the location of minerals first discovered? How is a mine constructed and operated? What different workers work in Colorado mines? How do mines help Colorado and our community? [Colorado, General, g. 3, p. 176]

Finding out how stone is quarried. Discussing the dependence of people upon workers in quarries for stone; discussing the dependence of stone workers upon people to buy their products. [South Dakota, Soc. Stu., g. 3, pp. 248–50]

Locate the great mining areas of the world. Find out why some of them are not being worked to any extent at the present time. List the different kinds of work associated with mining. (p. 89) Discuss: the capital required for mining; reserves for the future; substitutes for minerals; avoidance of waste; laws regulating the mineral industry. (pp. 83–5) [Fort Worth, Soc. Stu., g. 5]

Read about and discuss: the mining industry in the West; life in a mining town; the work of prospectors; the older and newer methods of mining. Arrange an exhibit of ores and objects made from them. Look up the location of oil fields in the West; the uses and importance of petroleum; how petroleum is transported. [Binghamton, Soc. Stu., g. 5, *Life and Work in the Great West*, pp. 20–2]

Make a collection of various kinds of coal. Report on the different qualities and uses of anthracite and bituminous coal. (p. 4) What are some of the hardships which miners experience? Try to have a miner exhibit his paraphernalia worn in the mines and explain the importance of each piece. Have him talk on the dangers of mining and the precautions taken. Make a diagram showing how hazards increase as depth increases. How is a child's life in a mining district different from the life of a child in Ossining? Correspond with boys and girls in a typical mining community. What is the government doing to improve the condition of miners? (pp. 2–3) [Ossining, N. Y., Soc. Stu., g. 6. *How the Miners of Coal and Iron Have Helped in the Development of Our Country*. Not tabulated.]

Topic 6. Lumbering; Forestry; Forest Products Including Rubber.
General: primary 9%; intermediate 54%. Social Studies: primary 10%; intermediate 67%.

Typically this topic indicates the more picturesque aspects of lumbering with comparatively little attention to such economic implications as the need of scientific forestry, the earnings and living conditions of lumbermen, and the selection and use of forest products. Sometimes the topic is limited to the growing and gathering of rubber.

LUMBERING: FORESTRY

Looking at pictures of lumber camps. Constructing a lumber camp. Discussing where lumbermen live and what they wear in the forests. Finding out how they know which trees to cut down. Collecting pictures of the different kinds of work done by lumbermen and sawmill workers. Finding out how close to the ground trees may be cut. Finding out what wages are paid to lumbermen. Playing lumber camp and impersonating the different workers. [South Dakota, Soc. Stu., g. 2, p. 123]

Find out and report to the class how long it takes northern pine, redwood, oak, and maple to become full grown. Find out what natural conditions help to make the Pacific coastal lands heavily wooded. Compare life and work in a western lumber camp, a southern camp, and a New York State camp. Discuss work at a saw mill and a planing mill. Discuss the duties of forest rangers and the value of their services. [Binghamton, Soc. Stu., g. 5, *Life and Work in the Great West,* p. 21]

Make a study of a lumber camp, its social conditions, its organization, division of labor, cutting operations, and the transportation of logs. Discuss wasteful cutting of forests. Visit a lumber yard. Note its organization to insure economy of labor and space. [Minnesota, General, g. 5, pp. 424–5]

Locate the forest belts on the map. Find out why some parts of our country have no forests. Tell how forests would help the people who live there. List the many uses of wood in our life today. List substitutes for wood. List the occupations furnished by the forests. List the factories in Hamilton County that manufacture things from forest products. What is meant by reforestation? What countries are ahead of us in forestry? [Hamilton County *Yearbook,* 1936–37, g. 6, pp. 126–8]

What is Europe doing in forestry? What is the United States doing? Discuss the future uses of forest products. [St. Paul, Soc. Stu., g. 6, pp. 5–6]

CONSUMER INTERESTS IN FOREST PRODUCTS

Identify timbers according to uses and grades. Inquire into methods of measuring lumber and the relative costs of different woods. [Minnesota, General, g. 5, pp. 424–5]

Collect samples of different qualities of rubber; separate according to quality or use. Learn how to care for rubber products. Learn how to patch an inner tube. [Washington, General, g. 6, p. 548]

Topic 7. The Fishing Industry.
General: primary 7%; intermediate 41%. Social Studies: primary 10%; intermediate 68%.

The fishing industry is usually taken up during the study of geography, and occurs most often on the fifth grade level. Such economic aspects as the use of fish in the diet and the international regulation of the industry are rarely treated.

What are some of the sea food resources of Chesapeake Bay? What is the value of the annual catch? Find out how the sea food of Maryland waters is conserved and protected by law. [Maryland, Science, g. 5, p. 146]

Make a graph showing the relative value of the fishing industry in various sections of the United States. Make a collection of products derived in whole or in part from fish and the fishing industries. Compile a chart showing the importance of the different kinds of fisheries in the United States, including value of annual catch, number of persons employed, amount of investment, and value of by-products. Dramatize a scene in a wholesale fish market. Plan typical sea food menus. Debate topics: Resolved: that fishing yields good returns for the money expended; that fishing laws violate personal liberty laws. Discuss the common rights of nations to use ocean waters for fishing. Hold a world fishing convention. [Fort Worth, Soc. Stu., g. 5, pp. 91–9]

Read about and discuss the salmon-fishing industry—habits of the fish, methods of catching and preserving, protection by the government. Visit a fish market and note the different kinds of fish offered for sale; list those caught on the Pacific Coast. [Binghamton, Soc. Stu., g. 5, *Life and Work in the Great West,* pp. 15–21]

Topic 8. Store-keeping.
General: primary 48%; intermediate 9%. Social Studies: primary 52%; intermediate 7%.

Playing store is one of the commonest activities in the primary grades. It involves numerous incidental learnings which may bear upon economic competence. More advanced study of store-keeping sometimes occurs on the intermediate level.

Construct a department store, divide into departments; make supplies for different departments. Play in the store. Discuss proper ways of buying in a department store, and rules of politeness toward clerks. [Utah, Soc. Stu., g. 1, pp. 5–8]

What people work in a grocery store and what does each do? How does the grocer keep the groceries clean and fresh? What equipment does he need? How does he get rid of his surplus goods? Why is it necessary for everyone who works in a grocery store to be courteous, honest, and clean? How are groceries paid for? (Cash, credit, or exchange) What does the grocer do with the money that is paid to him? Upon what workers does the grocer depend? [Missouri, General, g. 1, p. 866]

Visiting a grocery; talking with the grocer; watching grocery store advertisements and window displays. Playing store; making rules for courtesy in a store. Finding out how customers can help the grocer; how perishable foods are kept; how and why stores are inspected; how goods are sold (cash, telephone orders, delivery). Talking about purchasing wisely. [Brockton, Soc. Stu., g. 2, pp. 26–33]

Why can grocers accept a smaller margin of profit on a pound of sugar than on a pound of tea? Elementary meaning of overhead costs. Value in paying cash as opposed to charging. Losses by poor accounts and by perishable products. Supervision of grocery store by health authorities, by inspector of weights and measures. Employment of boy in grocery; hour's pay, what he must know. [New York, Arithmetic, g. 4, pp. 69–70]

List the various items to be considered in the overhead of a grocery store. Report on rates of commission given sales people in different stores in the community. [Amarillo, Arithmetic, g. 6, p. 40]

Trace the development of the store. Discuss the kinds of stores we have today. Compare wholesale, retail, department, and chain stores as to the kinds of services they render and their value to the community. (p. 29) Find out how to get credit at the stores in Houston. How do the stores protect themselves against those who do not pay their bills? (p. 33) [Houston, Soc. Stu., high g. 6, unit 1]

Topic 9. The Recreation Industry; Travel for Recreation. Includes trips, tours, resorts, national and state park systems, and commercial recreations.
General: primary 5%; intermediate 37%. Social Studies: primary 7%; intermediate 44%.

The industrial aspects of this topic are indicated less often than the consumer aspects. While in some courses attention is directed to the business of attracting and entertaining tourists and to the motion picture industry, in most of them the topic merely describes various resorts with major emphasis on the national parks. How to plan a trip or vacation and compute its cost is occasionally indicated.

Raise the question why people travel and lead into a discussion of how and where caring for visitors has become an important business. Find out who pays for the advertisements in newspapers and magazines calling attention to the different recreational and health centers of the United States. List the ways in which the tourist industry benefits a city or town. Visit hotels to find out how the tourist business helps them. Read pamphlets describing the different national parks. Find out about the accommodations offered tourists in national parks. Find out why the national parks were created and who were responsible for their being created. Plan a tour; estimate the cost of taking it. [Fort Worth, Soc. Stu., g. 4, supplementary units, pp. 190–2]

What different kinds of recreation may be enjoyed in state and national parks? Make a study of the state park system and find out what the particular attraction is at each park. How have the opportunities for recreation been increased by conservation? [New York, Science, g. 5, p. 171]

Planning an automobile trip. Making an expense estimate, budgeting spending money for the trip, discussing liability and accident insurance; reading an insurance policy, inquiring about rates and amount. [Mississippi, General, p. 377, grade not specified]

Comparing the costs of different ways of spending a vacation. Comparing the cost of different trips. Planning vacations the cost of which falls within a certain sum. [Illinois, Arithmetic, g. 4–6, p. 31]

Plan a camping trip and find distance to a suitable place. Compute cost of tents, food, clothing, and equipment. [Muskogee, Arithmetic, g. 6, p. 185]

Topic 10. Local Occupations in General.
General: primary 30%; intermediate 12%. Social Studies: primary 33%; intermediate 10%.

The study of "community helpers," so common in the primary grades, is apparently designed in part to help in the child's occupational orientation. In directing attention to wages, training required, or working conditions, the samples below are superior to the average.

Find out about the protection offered the different community helpers. Find out what salaries are paid the various helpers. Estimate the living and other expenses of each, touching only on the few expenses considered necessary for wholesome living. [Texas, General, g. 2, pp. 65–7]

Asking different workers about their work; reporting these interviews. Dramatizing and pantomiming workers. Telling of necessity of health for workers. Seeing movies and pictures of workers. [Princeton, Illinois, Soc. Stu., g. 3]

Discussion of: industries represented by the children's fathers; training required by each worker for his present occupation. [Madison, Soc. Stu., g. 6, p. 50]

Computing wages: of clerks, cashiers, and delivery men in grocery stores and meat markets; of dressmakers, milliners, shoemakers, and employees in dry goods stores; of cooks, waiters, waitresses, and bus-boys in restaurants; of janitors, gardeners, chambermaids, laundresses, domestic labor. [Sacramento, Arithmetic, g. 5, pp. 49–50]

Find out how boys and girls earn money in Fort Worth. Discuss the hours of work, the return, the physical and mental advantages or disadvantages, and the possible future of these ways of earning money. Find out what adults in Fort Worth do for a living; discuss the variation in time and money spent for preparation; the differences in wage scales and hours of work. [Fort Worth, Arithmetic, g. 6, p. 250]

Topic 11. Construction Workers and the Construction Industry. General: primary 18%; intermediate 16%. Social Studies: primary 29%; intermediate 13%.

This topic most often deals with the various kinds of building workers. The following are typical materials.

Observe cement workers, carpenters, masons, painters, plasterers, plumbers, electricians, and paper hangers, noting what they do. [Indiana, Soc. Stu., g. 2, p. 43]

Find out the kinds of workers who helped build the house you live in. Which of these kinds of workers have to be experts in their line, and which are laborers who take directions from others? [Houston, Soc. Stu., g. 3, unit 1, p. 57]

Invite friends or relatives engaged in construction work to talk to the class. Desired outcomes: (1) an appreciation of the contribution to the world's work made by child's own friend or relative; (2) realization of our dependence upon one another for our daily needs. [Berkeley, Soc. Stu., g. 4, p. 458]

Learn about the risks and condition of workers in the building trades. [Missouri, General, g. 4, p. 908]

Computing wages of carpenters, bricklayers, and other building artisans. [Sacramento, Arithmetic, g. 5, p. 49]

Topic 12. Electric Power. Its sources and importance; its value in the home, on the farm, and in industry.
General: primary 2%; intermediate 21%. Social Studies: primary 4%; intermediate 33%.

Typically this important topic is limited to a brief description of how streams are harnessed to produce electricity. The possibilities of greatly increasing the production and use of electricity, and what that may mean to society are sometimes indicated. The question of the ownership or control of the production and transmission of electricity is sometimes mentioned. (See topic 55, p. 144.)

Look at pictures of big generators. Find out what kinds of power are used in turning generators in power plants. (g. 4, p. 87) Find out how and where the electricity used in your home and school building was produced. Find out the cost of current per kilowatt hour in your vicinity and learn how to figure the cost of running different electrical devices. (g. 6, p. 101) [New York, Science]

Find out what three cents' worth of electricity will do for you. Discuss the importance of electricity to civilization. [Iowa, Science, g. 4–6, p. 76]

Find out why some homes use electricity and others do not. Make a list of the ways people use electricity. [Iowa, Geography, g. 3, p. 69]

Topics to consider: The new dams in the Columbia River; what will be their effect on the food supply? On power rates? Other power dams. Municipal power and light plants. [Washington, Soc. Stu., g. 4–6, p. 9]

Outline of content: Meaning and generation of hydroelectric power; need for a constant flow of water; why New England has developed a greater part of its potential water power than any other section; effect of the use of hydroelectric power in locating manufacturing plants; development of water power in the southern Appalachians and in the West; combined use of water and coal in generating power; value of a network of electric transmission lines, the use of water power as a means of conserving other power resources. [Denver, Soc. Stu., g. 6, pp. 132–3]

Reading about and discussing the production and use of electricity. Making a survey of homes to determine the extent of the use of electricity, and the cost of electricity to the homes. Investigating the services rendered by the Tennessee Valley Authority and the Rural Electrification Administration. [Mississippi, General, g. 6, pp. 264–9]

What states have large amounts of developed water power? What states can develop much more? Why ought more water power to be developed and used? What use is made of the power from most of the large water-power plants? [Massachusetts, Science, g. 5, p. 72]

COMMENTS ON GROUP I

This group includes the two topics which appear most frequently of the entire fifty-six, namely "Farming" and "Transportation." Of the seven topics appearing in more than 50 per cent of the courses tabulated, this group has four—"Farming," "Transportation," "Manufacturing," and "Communication." Only two topics in the group, "Construction Workers" and "Electric Power Industry," appear in fewer courses than the median topic, which appears in 19.5 per cent, and these two are only slightly below the median. Numerically it is clear that "Industries and Occupations" is the most important of the seven groups of topics.

The higher frequency of "Farming," "Transportation," "Manufacturing," and "Communication" compared to the other topics in this group is partly due to their tendency to occur on both the primary and the intermediate level. The other topics tend to occur only on the primary or only on the intermediate level. "Local Occupations in General" and "Storekeeping" are found chiefly in primary courses, probably because they lend themselves to dramatic play. "Fishing," "Lumbering," and "Mining" are found almost entirely in the intermediate courses, probably because in most localities they must be studied from books.

Since the topic "Planning and Constructing a House" (see Table II) is eighth in rank, it is surprising to find that "Construction Workers" should be twenty-ninth. The former is usually associated with the activity of building a play house, an activity which would gain in reality and value if supplemented by consideration of how construction workers build a real house.

It is interesting to note that the recreation industry, on which one-seventh of the national income is spent, ranks twenty-fourth in the list of topics. Nor is it developed to any considerable extent in the courses in which it does occur. Its low rank and scant content can hardly be due to any lack of interest on the part of children.

The importance of the electric power industry and its great potentialities for the betterment of living would seem to warrant a consideration equal to that of other industries taught in the intermediate grades.

However, it ranks at the bottom of the twelve topics in the Industries and Occupations group, being included in only 15 per cent of the courses, and even in these, with but two or three exceptions, receiving scant attention. To an imaginative teacher of intermediate grades the topic probably presents no greater difficulty than "Communication," or "Mining" in an area remote from mines.

As to content of topics in this group, some of the better samples of which are presented on pp. 62–78, the following may be said:

1. In the study of an industry the majority of courses give nearly all their attention to mere description of processes, and little or no attention to the selection and use of the product, and to opportunities for employment, earnings, and working conditions in the industry. As outlined in most courses, the study of an industry would contribute practically nothing either to consumer education or to occupational orientation.

2. There is a strong tendency to describe industries as if they were static. Very few courses direct attention to additional services that the industry may in future render to society through greater and better output, a wider distribution of the output, more attention to conservation, and better provision for its employees.

3. In the majority of courses the suggestions for teaching industries and occupations center around make-believe activities and the reading of textbooks. Many courses suggest playing grocery store but few suggest excursions to real stores to observe, to interview the storekeeper, and to make real purchases. Similarly, nearly all courses propose reading about the fishing industry, but hardly any propose finding out how the streams of the community could be made once more to teem with fish.

4. The more nearly the content is related to the real experiences and observations of the children, as distinguished from book study and make-believe activities, the greater is its bearing on economic competence. In those courses which recommend first-hand study of an occupation or enterprise, it is fairly usual for attention to be directed to such functional aspects as the selection of the product, the use of by-products, the training and skill of the workers, working conditions, and the importance of raw materials, the investment of capital, good transportation facilities, and a market for the output. When, however,

the content is to be developed wholly or largely from books, it tends to be more highly generalized and therefore has less application to the experiences of the children and adults of the community.

5. The more nearly the content is related to the actual experiences and observations of the children, the less can it avoid dealing with the unsolved problems of the community, such as the need for conserving the soil or the forests, for better transportation, communication, and electric-transmission facilities, for more employment, new enterprises, and the like.

GROUP II. HOME LIFE IN OUR COMMUNITY

Each of the thirteen topics in this group occurs in 124 courses on the average, or 30 per cent of the total. Numerically the group is the second most important channel of education for economic competence in the elementary school.

The topics deal with (1) the selection, care, and use of food, clothing, shelter, furnishings, playthings, household preparations, remedies and treatments, and (2) the practice of hospitality, embodying both household arts and consumer education insofar as they are taught in the first six grades. More than any other, this group may be expected to contribute to the *consumer* phases, as distinguished from the *vocational* and *citizenship* phases, of economic competence.

Evidence as to the place of household arts and consumer education in the elementary school includes the following items:

1. Analysis of the declared objectives of elementary courses of study. (See pp. 48–50)

2. Table II, showing the number of general and social studies courses in which each topic in this group appears. (See p. 81)

3. Samples of course of study materials selected to indicate the range of each topic's activities and problems with a bearing on economic competence. (See pp. 83–96)

4. Table VI, Money Management, in which certain related topics appear. (See p. 132)

5. Table XI, Topics Found in Science Courses, of which the group "Household Science" is closely related to consumer education. (See p. 157)

TABLE II

HOME LIFE IN OUR COMMUNITY

Topics Related to Economic Competence Found in General and Social Studies Courses

NUMBER AND PER CENT OF COURSES IN WHICH TOPIC APPEARS *

TOPIC	COMBINED COURSES (420)		GENERAL COURSES (210)								SOCIAL STUDIES COURSES (210)							
	No.	%	1	2	3	4	5	6	Total	%	1	2	3	4	5	6	Total	%
			Grades								Grades							
13. Diet: selecting a healthful ..	249	59	27	30	28	26	27	26	164	78	25	19	19	9	7	6	85	41
14. House: planning and constructing	174	41	29	18	16	12	9	8	92	44	28	13	21	6	8	6	82	39
15. Clothing: selection of	167	40	25	23	23	17	19	16	123	59	14	6	14	5	3	2	44	21
16. Sewing, mending, or dyeing	149	36	17	14	14	17	12	13	87	41	17	16	12	6	6	5	62	30
17. House: caring for and improving	148	35	24	10	13	14	10	11	82	39	26	9	16	4	7	4	66	31
18. House: furnishing and decorating	145	35	23	17	13	12	14	12	91	43	26	7	9	4	5	3	54	26
19. Food: actual preparation or preservation of	134	32	12	15	12	8	8	4	59	28	25	16	16	7	8	3	75	36
20. Clothing: care of	121	29	17	19	12	12	9	10	79	38	14	9	12	4	2	1	42	20
21. Textiles: kinds, selection of	92	22	7	5	8	7	9	7	43	20	6	10	19	7	3	4	49	23
22. Refreshments: actual serving to guests	83	20	9	12	8	7	1	2	39	19	19	8	9	3	4	1	44	21
23. Toys: care, repair, making, selection of	72	17	18	15	9	3	7	6	58	28	9	4	1	0	0	0	14	7
24. Remedies and treatments: selection of	40	10	5	5	3	7	9	8	37	18	1	0	1	0	1	0	3	1
25. Household preparations	39	9	0	0	4	7	4	1	16	8	4	3	7	3	4	2	23	11

* A course is the program for a single grade. For each grade 35 general courses and 35 social studies courses were tabulated.

COUNTING THE THIRTEEN TOPICS IN GROUP II

According to a decision, explained on p. 29, no difference in counting was made between activities and topics that are merely suggested and those that appear in the recommended subject matter of a course. This decision had more effect on the count for Group II than for any other group, and particularly affected the count of the topics "Sewing, mending, or dyeing," "Food: actual preparation or preservation of," "Refreshments: actual serving to guests," "Toys," insofar as their repair or construction is indicated, and the "Household preparations." In most courses these topics occur as suggested incidental activities. For example, dyeing cloth with natural dyes and making Indian costumes may be suggested as part of a unit on Indians; making soap as part of a unit on colonial or pioneer life; making butter, custard, and cottage cheese as part of a unit on dairying. In view of the practical difficulties in carrying out such activities, particularly in a large class of primary children, it may be doubted that they are as often carried out as are other suggestions and recommendations found in a given course of study.

Assuming that these suggested activities are actually carried out, it must be admitted that their primary objective is not, in most courses of study, to teach sewing, dyeing, cooking, or the selection and use of soap. Nevertheless, it seems reasonable to assume that they will yield a certain amount of information or skill that has value for consumer education. A teacher who is conscious of the consumer values involved will find that experiences of this sort provide excellent opportunity to interest and instruct children in basic consumer skills and understandings.

Apart from the question of what to do with suggested activities, counting of the topics in Group II proved simple. The only topic that gave trouble was Topic 24, "Selection of remedies and treatments." Many courses make provision for explaining to children the necessity for the yearly health inspection by the school doctor; it was decided not to count this, but to count any attempt to direct attention to the problem of selecting from the different types of practitioners and cultists, or to the need of systematic medical and dental care. With respect to remedies, discussion of how to select supplies for a home medicine cabinet, and the advisability of avoiding advertised remedies in self-medication was counted, but not such specific information as "use boric acid solution for bathing the eyes."

MATERIALS FROM COURSES OF STUDY ILLUSTRATING THE CONTENT OF
TOPICS IN GROUP II LIKELY TO CONTRIBUTE TO ECONOMIC COMPETENCE

Topic 13. Selecting a Healthful Diet. Value of milk, eggs, fruit, green vegetables, cod liver oil, etc. Selecting a lunch.
General: primary 81%; intermediate 75%. Social Studies: primary 60%; intermediate 21%.

This topic is found in 59 per cent of the general and social studies courses tabulated. Its development varies from a mere discussion of the value of milk to a lengthy study of all the essential classes of nutrients. The comparative costs of various menus and foodstuffs are seldom treated, and in this respect some of the samples below are considerably better than average.

Make a list of foods that help boys and girls to build good teeth, strong bones, and muscles. Discuss how our diet should differ in summer and winter. [Houston, Soc. Stu., g. 3, unit 1, pp. 30–3]

Discovering why milk is so important in the diet through reading and class discussion. An experiment may be made with two white mice, one receiving and one not receiving milk. Arranging a bulletin board showing the many ways to use milk. [Mississippi, General, g. 3, pp. 172–3]

What is the cost of milk as compared with all other types of food? What is the cost per pound of different cereals, vegetables, and fruits? How would you select a good yet inexpensive diet? [Washington, General, g. 1–3, pp. 502–3]

Write a menu for a week showing a balanced diet. Discuss school lunches to find out what constitutes a wholesome lunch. Keep for one week a list of the foods purchased in the school cafeteria by each pupil; do they represent a well-balanced diet? [Houston, Soc. Stu., g. 5, unit 3, p. 16]

Finding the costs of various lunches. Making a record of daily lunches bought and the cost. Finding the average amount spent weekly for soup or vegetables, milk, fruit, and sweets. [Mississippi, General, p. 375, grade not specified]

Finding out the minerals obtained in our foods, and their value. [San Mateo County, Soc. Stu., g. 5, p. 136]

Discussing why cod liver oil and vegetables are now considered so important for the health of growing children. Inviting a dentist to talk on the effects of a proper diet upon teeth. Experimenting with animals to show effects of improper food upon health and growth. [Virginia, General, g. 5, p. 151]

Planning wholesome, inexpensive meals. Substituting inexpensive dishes for more expensive ones. Planning picnic lunches and refreshments for parties. [Sacramento, Arithmetic, g. 5, p. 49]

Review the contributions of fruit to health and the value of vegetables in the diet. Keep individual diaries of vegetables eaten. Write letters to children of different lands asking about their diets. Discuss the value of sweets in the diet, the time to eat sweets, the amount to eat, the most desirable kinds. Plan meatless menus emphasizing the value of dairy products and eggs. Make menus showing the comparative costs of food, and emphasizing the low cost of milk. [Binghamton, Soc. Stu., g. 6, *How Agriculture Supplies Our Needs and Wants,* pp. 15–28]

Topic 14. Planning and Constructing a House. Kinds and uses of rooms. Materials used in building. The housing problem.
General: primary 60%; intermediate 28%. Social Studies: primary 59%; intermediate 19%.

Typically this topic centers in the building of a play- house, supplemented perhaps by an excursion to see a house under construction. Emphasis is laid on the uses of the various rooms, the materials of which houses are made, and the value of sunlight, air, and attractiveness in a house. The cost of shelter, the causes and effects of bad housing, and government efforts to meet the housing problem are rare items.

THE MATERIALS AND DESIGN OF A HOUSE

Building and furnishing a play house. Discussing: the materials of which houses are made, health provisions, and general attractiveness. Objective: ability to explain the uses and conveniences of various rooms in the house and the health value of proper lighting, heating, and ventilation. [San Mateo County, Soc. Stu., g. 1, pp. 32–4]

Visit: lumber and brick yards, displays of building materials, buildings under construction. Develop the story of the evolution of the modern house. [Indiana, Soc. Stu., g. 2, pp. 43–5]

Find out why concrete blocks and bricks are being used more today than formerly. If you could choose a house, would you take one of wood or of brick? Why? [Iowa, Geography, g. 3, pp. 66–7]

To build up concepts of materials used in building a house, bring in samples of wood showing various grains, kinds of building stone, bricks, tile, nails, screws, locks, and hinges; make a concrete block, a hollow cement block, an adobe brick; mix plaster and demonstrate its use on a framework of laths; mix mortar and demonstrate its use with bricks. [Denver, Soc. Stu., g. 4, pp. 71–2]

List the different ways in which warmth, coolness, sanitation, and fire-proofing may be provided for in building a house. Compare the price of a house built of lumber and one built of brick; reasons for difference. Draw floor plans for a house. [Houston, Soc. Stu., g. 3, unit 1, pp. 57–8]

THE HOUSING PROBLEM

What are minimum standards for a good home? What can our communities do to make houses measure up to these standards? What are the effects and the causes of poor housing? What are our resources for good housing? Prepare an assembly program on housing and an exhibit of housing models, posters, and graphs. [Missouri, General, g. 4, pp. 908–11]

Discuss what one wishes to buy when he buys a home. (Protection, safety, privacy, space, proper location with respect to work, possibilities of comfort and beauty.) What are the minimum housing standards that every person in the United States has a right to demand? Estimate the cost of different types of houses today, securing figures from persons who have built recently. Summarize the causes of poor housing conditions. Discuss the house of the future, new materials and methods of construction; trademarked houses; new architectural designs, such as the Dymaxion house. [Fort Worth, Soc. Stu., g. 5, pp. 133–41]

Talk to your doctor, a policeman, and your parents about the effect of slums upon the people who live in them, and how they cost your parents. Find out what is being done by the national government to abolish slums in Atlanta. [Atlanta, Soc. Stu., *Living and Growing in the Home-School-Community; grades 4, 5, 6,* g. 5, p. 41. Not tabulated]

Topic 15. Selecting Clothing. Choosing clothes appropriate for various kinds of weather; choosing clothes suitable for school, for play, and for a party; choosing clothes that are durable; choosing clothes that are beautiful and becoming.
General: primary 68%; intermediate 50%. Social Studies: primary 32%; intermediate 10%.

Typically this topic involves only the discussion of clothes suitable for various kinds of weather and clothes appropriate for school wear.

Consideration of how to select clothing for low cost and durability is sometimes indicated. How to select clothes for beauty and becomingness is provided for in 26 per cent of the general courses and in 8 per cent of the social studies courses tabulated.

STANDARDS IN DRESS

Show how clothing is made beautiful through the choice of suitable material, color, pattern or design, and texture. Stress appropriateness of cotton textiles for certain purposes, silk for other purposes. (g. 1) Discuss the articles of clothing the children wear at school, at home, when visiting. Visit a store, ask questions concerning the cost of clothing articles and materials, notice the price tags, select and buy materials for doll clothes. (g. 2, pp. 888–9) [South Dakota, General]

Observe the effect of placing a white cloth and a black cloth on the snow in direct sunlight. The snow will melt much faster under the dark cloth. Why? Light-colored clothes are cooler than dark-colored clothes when worn in sunlight. Why? [New York, Science, g. 4, pp. 91–2]

Make lists of clothing needed by a boy or girl in the fourth grade. Discuss the relationship between clothing and health. Determine what constitutes beauty in clothing. Draw dresses you would consider good taste for school, a party, winter sports, a camp, etc. Plan a contest in judging costumes for boys and girls with reference to their harmony and fitness for wearing on given occasions. Give a style show portraying appropriate clothing for different occasions. [Fort Worth, Soc. Stu., g. 4, pp. 158–61]

Experiment to discover becoming colors in costumes. Set up standards for selecting clothing. Plan appropriate dresses for various occasions. [Texas, General, g. 5, pp. 57–60]

Bring in all types of costume accessories for boys and girls; examine these for ideas, design, color, and methods of construction. Visit a department store and a limited price store to see accessories. Design and make accessories, working out the color scheme to harmonize with the costume with which it is to be worn. Display costumes with accessories at a P. T. A. meeting. [Texas, *Tentative Course of Study for Years One to Six*, g. 6, p. 309. Not tabulated]

SELECTION OF SHOES AND LEATHER GOODS

Visit a shoe repair shop to see crude leather. Visit a luggage shop to see kinds of leather used in bags and to learn of durability and cost. Make a booklet showing the uses of leather and the process of making leather. [Madison, Soc. Stu., g. 3, pp. 17–8]

Make a pedograph and decide what features a shoe should have to fit the foot. Visit a shoe store, observe shoes of suitable design, and listen to discussion of the points of a good shoe by a salesman. Look at foot in shoe as shown by fluoroscope and decide if shoe fits correctly. Collect pictures of good and bad shoes. Make a list of the important points to remember in buying shoes. [Texas, *Tentative Course of Study for Years One to Six*, g. 4-6, pp. 423-4. Not tabulated]

Collect samples of kinds of leather and imitation leather. Study methods of adulteration and use of substitutes for leather. Take an old shoe or glove apart; note parts, shapes, how assembled. [Washington, General, g. 5, p. 549]

Topic 16. Sewing, Dyeing, or Mending.
General: primary 43%; intermediate 40%. Social Studies: primary 43%; intermediate 16%.

Typically this topic occurs as a suggested activity in connection with building and furnishing a doll house where the making of doll clothes and doll house furnishings is indicated, and in connection with giving a play or puppet show where the making of costumes is indicated. In some courses for intermediate grades, lessons in sewing and mending are suggested as a part of the work in industrial arts. In one course (Boston) regular lessons in sewing are indicated for girls in grades four through six.

Make clothes for a doll. Cut patterns from paper, select appropriate materials and colors, cut, and sew seams with running stitch. Compare with clothes needed for a child. [Washington, General, g. 1, p. 525]

Make curtains, cushions, and chair covers for the play house. (g. 1, p. 50) Cut paper patterns for and make work aprons. Make winter clothing for dolls. (g. 2, pp. 127-8) [South Dakota, Soc. Stu.]

Mend some woolen articles. Darn stockings. Sew on buttons. Knit wash cloths. Make Indian costumes. [New Hampshire, General, g. 3-4, p. 163]

Smaller children can make rag dolls and dress them. They can make curtains, sheets, furniture covers, etc., for a doll house. Older children can design and make costumes for plays and special occasions. Children can make tea towels, dust cloths, hot-dish mats, scarfs, luncheon sets, etc. for home use. Both boys and girls can learn to sew on buttons, darn hose, mend, and patch. [Virginia, General, g. 1-6, p. 311]

Topic 17. Caring for and Improving a Home. Lighting and heating, selecting fuel, installing conveniences, making ornamental plantings, making a flower garden, painting the exterior. General: primary 45%; intermediate 33%. Social Studies: primary 49%; intermediate 14%.

In the primary grades this topic usually centers about the care of a playhouse; in the intermediate grades it usually occurs in outlines in hygiene and science. The comparative heating values of various fuels is an uncommon item.

Topics which might be discussed and activities which might be carried out in a playhouse unit: proper method of airing and making beds, of sweeping, dusting, and ventilating rooms, of washing, drying, and putting away dishes, of caring for sink, woodwork, and paint. [Washington, General, g. 1, p. 524]

Make excursions to see attractive homes, photograph beauty spots around them. Discuss plans for beautifying homes. Each child may discuss what he wants to do, such as: make a flower garden, plant vines, paint a fence. Make photographs before and after the home is improved. [Texas, General, g. 4, pp. 36–7]

Discussion of painting of houses and number of gallons of paint used. Figuring the cost of painting, of shingles, of grass and flower seeds. [Springfield, Arithmetic, g. 3, p. 3]

Make a graph to show the relative heating values of common fuels. Compare the costs. [Fort Worth, Arithmetic, g. 6, p. 303]

Discussing the heating value of soft wood compared to hard wood, and of both compared to coal. Discussing the way wood should be arranged in a stove so that the fire will burn well. Comparing different kinds of coal and coke. [San Mateo County, Science, g. 5, pp. 90–1]

Is the same kind of light and heat used in all our homes? Where do the different kinds of fuels come from? What does it cost to keep my home warm and well lighted? Does heat and light for a home cost more or less now than long ago? Write to any company which may offer information on articles used for heating and lighting. (Among the desired outcomes: understanding that modern ways of heating and lighting are safer and more healthful than the old ways, probably adding years to our lives.) [Brockton, Soc. Stu., g. 3, pp. 30–41]

Collect plans and pictures of homes and study arrangements for lighting and ventilating. Is your home well lighted? Find out how your home is ventilated. [New York, Science, g. 6, p. 174]

Discuss the purpose of fuses. [Iowa, Science, g. 3, p. 76]

How do colored bulbs change the light? How does the shade change the light? What kind of shade is best for reading purposes? Do light walls and furnishings brighten a room? [Montana, Science, g. 3, pp. 4–5]

Topic 18. Furnishing and Decorating the Interior of a Home. Selecting, remodeling, or arranging furniture; choosing decorative materials and objects; finishing the interior.
General: primary 50%; intermediate 36%. Social Studies: primary 40%; intermediate 11%.

In the primary grades this topic is often indicated in connection with building a playhouse; and in the intermediate grades it is often indicated as part of the content in art. The materials do not always appear to be related to the furnishing and decorating problems of families of average and below-average income.

Find pictures of furniture to illustrate how a house is furnished. Plan how to furnish a doll's house; how to make the rugs, curtains, bed linen, table covers. [Fort Worth, Soc. Stu., g. 1, pp. 33–4]

To build up concepts of materials used in decorating and furnishing homes, bring samples of wood used in furniture, samples of paint colors, samples of materials used in rug-making. [Denver, Soc. Stu., g. 4, p. 71]

Construct furniture for various rooms, studying the woods, cloth, leather, and their sources. Study the origin and making of carpets, rugs, and draperies. Secure from lumber yard or a new house woods used for interior trim. Stain the woods to harmonize with various color schemes. [Connecticut, Science, ungraded, pp. 90–1]

Examine samples of beautiful wallpaper to note the fine workmanship used in the design, the nice use of color, and the quality of the paper upon which it is printed. [Houston, Soc. Stu., g. 3, p. 59]

Collect pictures of different kinds of carpet materials. Examine carpets to see differences in pile and in way colors are carried. Make drawings to show construction of weave. Compare carpets and Oriental rugs. Find out how Oriental rugs are made. [Washington, General, g. 6, p. 555]

Using advertisements in newspaper, figure the cost of moderate-priced furnishings for a home, room by room. [Amarillo, Arithmetic, g. 6, p. 40]

Children made a list of electrical appliances used in homes, estimated the cost of each and the total amount spent by a family on electrical appliances. [Springfield, Arithmetic, g. 6, p. 32]

Topic 19. Actual Preparation or Preservation of Foods.
General: primary 37%; intermediate 19%. Social Studies: primary 54%; intermediate 17%.

The preparation or preservation of a few foods is found as a suggested activity in many primary and some intermediate courses of study.

Make vegetable soup for the school lunch to learn the methods of cleaning and preparing vegetables. Make ice cream and baked custard. Can beans or apples by the cold pack method. Dry apples, peaches, and beans. Make jelly from fruit. [Florida, General, g. 2, pp. 110–1]

Make some important milk foods, such as custard, cocoa, butter, cheese, cream soups, ice cream, milk shakes. Discuss recipes for important milk foods. [Mississippi, General, g. 2, pp. 170–3]

Under the problem "How does the farmer prepare for winter?" the following activities are recommended: (*a*) make apple sauce, apple butter, apple or cranberry jelly, (*b*) dry apples, (*c*) wrap apples in tissue paper for storage, (*d*) preserve eggs in water glass or glycerine, (*e*) salt a jar of cut beans, (*f*) bury carrots in sand, (*g*) can tomatoes, (*h*) dry beans or peas in bags, (*i*) wrap cabbages in paper to store in a cool cellar, (*j*) bury some vegetables in a pit in the school yard. Baking cookies or muffins, popping corn, churning butter, and making cottage cheese, ice cream, and cocoa are designated as essential learnings in this same unit. [Missouri, General, g. 2, p. 869]

Make bread, cookies, and biscuits. Figure the cost. [St. Louis County, Soc. Stu., g. 2 or 3, p. 108]

Try to make olive oil, raisins, peanut butter, dried cocoanut, macaroni. Prepare and serve a colonial dinner. Experiment with various ways of preserving food, such as salting, smoking, drying, pickling, burying, preserving with sugar. [Washington, General, g. 5, p. 544]

Cooking vegetables in a waterless cooker and with water to show that too much water destroys some of the food values. [Virginia, General, g. 5, p. 151]

Make fruit candy; find out why this is better than sugar candy. Prepare and serve lunch from food products of the West. [Binghamton, Soc. Stu., g. 5, *Life and Work in the Great West*, pp. 20–3]

Topic 20. Care of Clothing. Airing, hanging, keeping clean, laundering, protecting from moths.
General: primary 46%; intermediate 30%. Social Studies: primary 33%; intermediate 7%.

Frequently this topic is limited to a discussion of the importance of hanging wraps and keeping one's clothes clean. Occasionally it deals with methods of laundering, dry cleaning, and protection from moths. The care of shoes and rubber goods is sometimes indicated.

Discuss the care necessary for the cleanliness and longer life of clothing. [Kansas City, Soc. Stu., g. 2, p. 119]

Wash wool in warm soapy water; do not squeeze. Desired outcome: knowledge of the correct way to wash and care for woolen garments. [Washington, General, g. 3, p. 535]

Wash one piece of wool in warm water, another in boiling water, to notice the difference in the size and softness of the pieces. [Houston, Soc. Stu., g. 3, unit 1, p. 43]

Remove grease spots from various materials with various dry cleansers. Find out why we should exercise great care in using dry cleansers. Read advertisements concerning soaps. Try several soaps, including lye soap, on various materials several times each; observe results. Remove iron rust, orange juice, and various stains from different fabrics. [Texas, General, g. 4, pp. 47–9]

Learning how moths destroy woolen materials, furs, feathers, etc. Learning when they lay their eggs. [San Mateo County, Science, g. 5, p. 64]

Learn the best ways to take care of each kind of material. Discuss methods of cleaning clothes. Remove ink stains from cloth. Make posters showing right and wrong ways to treat clothing. [Fort Worth, Soc. Stu., g. 4, pp. 158–60]

Write a story about how to make shoes last longer. [Houston, Soc. Stu., g. 3, unit 1, p. 48]

Experiment with cleaning agents on leather. [Washington, General, g. 5, p. 549]

Find out about the proper care of rubber goods for durability. [Madison, Soc. Stu., g. 3, p. 41]

Topic 21. The Kinds of Textiles. Their properties and selection. General: primary 19%; intermediate 22%. Social Studies: primary 33%; intermediate 13%.

Typically this topic provides only for learning some of the common fabrics by name. Occasionally it treats the properties of textiles, their adaptability to various uses, and their comparative prices. Sometimes it includes simple tests useful in purchasing textiles and articles made from textiles.

CHARACTERISTICS OF TEXTILE FIBERS AND OF TEXTILES

Collect different kinds of plant fibers and kinds of cloth made from them. Examine your own clothes and find out if they came from plants and from what plants they came. Examine plant fibers and samples of cloth with a microscope. [New York, Science, g. 3, p. 162]

Collecting samples of cotton fabrics; organizing, mounting, and labeling these for a cotton sample book. Learning the uses of various cotton fabrics. Finding out what accounts for their differences in texture. [Los Angeles County, Soc. Stu., g. 5, p. 204]

Making a list of things made from wool. Collecting samples of woolen materials and classifying them according to design, plaid, stripes, diagonals, and repeated patterns. [Vancouver, Soc. Stu., g. 3, pp. 27–8]

Why does linen make better towels than cotton? Which wears longer, linen or cotton materials? [Montgomery County, Science, g. 2, p. 5]

Examining a piece of linen to find the characteristics of flax fiber in comparison with cotton. (p. 75) Comparing linen and cotton to see which material absorbs more moisture. (Dishes may be wiped on each; note that linen makes glasses shine.) Dye some wool to see if it takes color readily. Testing the strength of fibers taken from cotton, linen, and rayon materials. Burning little pieces of wool, linen, silk, cotton, and rayon. Examining cotton, linen, or rayon materials to see if the materials were dyed in the piece, or if the threads were dyed before weaving. (pp. 80–1) [San Mateo County, Science, g. 5]

Find out why wool is so much warmer than cotton. Discuss the relative merits of silk and rayon. Learn to distinguish fabrics made of wool, cotton, linen, and silk. Make charts or booklets showing kinds of clothing made from wool, cotton, linen, and silk. Find out the difference between printed and woven designs. Make a collection of textiles to show different patterns, noting whether they are printed or woven designs. [Fort Worth, Soc. Stu., g. 4, pp. 146–8]

Collect samples of different textiles. Examine these with a magnifying glass to determine differences in texture and weaving. [Binghamton, Soc. Stu., g. 6, *How Agriculture Supplies Our Needs and Wants*, p. 24]

SELECTING TEXTILES FOR COST AND SUITABILITY

Visiting a dry goods store to find the cost of woolen materials compared to the cost of other materials. [Vancouver, Soc. Stu., g. 3, p. 28]

Finding out what factors enter into the cost of cotton cloth. [Los Angeles County, Soc. Stu., g. 5, p. 204]

List all the materials used in clothing. Compare the values of these materials, considering cost, looks, wearing qualities, etc. [Colorado, Science, g. 6, pp. 463–4]

Measuring amount of material needed for various garments. Selecting the least expensive and most serviceable materials. [Sacramento, Arithmetic, g. 5, p. 49]

Determine why the price of material varies; compare the cost of cotton, linen, woolen, and silk goods. Discuss the cost of all wool and of mixed wool and cotton goods. When would the mixture be satisfactory? [Fort Worth, Soc. Stu., g. 4, pp. 146–8]

TESTS APPLICABLE IN PURCHASING TEXTILES

Testing the firmness of weave by holding fabric in both hands and pressing down on it with both thumbs. Testing materials for shrinkage and for fading when exposed to sunlight. Examining cotton materials to see if sizing is used. Examining materials to see if cotton or linen threads are used and to see how much cotton is mixed with the linen. (pp. 80–2) Examining materials to see if they are all wool or part wool and part cotton. (p. 64) [San Mateo County, Science, g. 5]

Finding out how we can tell the difference between pure wool or pure linen and the cotton imitations or adulterations of these fabrics. [Los Angeles County, Soc. Stu., g. 5, p. 204]

Learn to identify silk and to test silk for weighting by burning a sample. [Madison, Soc. Stu., g. 3, p. 59]

Topic 22. Practicing Hospitality Involving the Serving of Refreshments.
General: primary 28%; intermediate 10%. Social Studies: primary 34%; intermediate 8%.

The typical example of this topic occurs as a suggestion for planning and giving a tea or luncheon at school for mothers, or planning and giving a party at school for another class. Planning a suitable menu at minimum cost is, one can safely assume, a problem usually involved in this activity. The activity may also afford experience in purchasing and preparing the refreshments.

Plan a Valentine Day program and invite the mothers; serve refreshments and deliver valentines to the guests. [Texas, General, g. 2, p. 71]

Plan a birthday or holiday party. List the materials needed for refreshments, decorations, and games. Find the cost of the separate items and the total. [Muskogee, Arithmetic, g. 4, p. 144]

Having a party at which typical Dutch food is served, such as bread with butter (churned by the class), cheese, and cocoa. Purchasing materials for costumes and supplies for the party. [Muncie, General, g. 3, pp. 136-7]

Topic 23. Toys. Their care and repair; their selection; the actual making of toys.
General: primary, 40%; intermediate, 15%. Social Studies: primary, 13%; intermediate 0%.

Discussion of the care of toys and the making and repair of toys is frequently indicated. Consideration of how to select toys is sometimes indicated.

Collecting and exhibiting toys. Looking at toy displays in windows. Collecting pictures of toys from advertisements. Visiting a toy shop; observing prices and arrangement. Visiting a fire station to watch the men repairing toys. Collecting materials and making toys. Exhibiting toys made. Conducting a toy store. Understandings to be secured: Expensive toys are not necessary for fun; durable, washable toys are better values than fragile toys; children owe the storekeeper care in handling toys on display; much pleasure can be given by the repair of used toys for poor children. [Madison, Soc. Stu., g. 1, pp. 26-36]

Old toys were collected, mended, repainted, and given to needy children through the Red Cross. [Atlanta, Soc. Stu., *Living and Growing in the Home-School Community: Grades 1, 2, 3,* g. 1, pp. 39-41. Not tabulated]

During a discussion of how children can amuse themselves, the making of playthings was suggested. It was decided to make things from waste materials which could be gathered from school and home. The children made ring toss and bean bag games, doll furniture, puzzles, and paper dolls. [Denver, Soc. Stu., g. 1, p. 65]

Bring advertisements of Christmas toys. Discuss the selection of suitable toys. Notice difference between a well-made toy and one that isn't well-made, between a toy that has been taken care of and one that has not. (g. 1, unit 3.) Bring toys to school to study cost, durability, workmanship, and appropriateness for gifts. (g. 3, unit 3) [Amarillo, General, no paging]

Topic 24. Selection of Remedies and Treatments. Why, when, and from whom to seek medical or dental care. Selection of supplies for a home medicine cabinet.

General: primary 12%; intermediate 23%. Social Studies: primary 2%; intermediate 1%.

This topic occurs chiefly in outlines for health education, and is given very little space. No attempt is made to describe a reasonable program of medical and dental supervision for an average family. Practically no attempt is made to suggest how to select a physician or dentist. For other comments see pp. 82-3.

Construct a first aid cabinet for school or home and fill it with standard supplies. [Virginia, General, g. 6, p. 186]

Prepare a home medicine cabinet. List articles for use and learn the reason for including each. (g. 5, p. 218) Why see a dentist twice a year? (g. 4, p. 215) [Nevada, General, Vol. II]

Contrasting household remedies of today with those based upon superstitions of former times. Making a survey to discover remedies and practices based upon superstitions now in vogue. [Arkansas, General, g. 4-6, p. 134]

Gather labels of patent medicines. Read, noting contents and the many ailments for which they are recommended. (g. 4, p. 47) Write the American Medical Association for materials on their investigation of quacks and nostrums. (g. 4-6, p. 91) [Texas, General]

Understandings to be developed: Take medicine only on advice of physician. Seek only accepted scientific professional services in the treatment of disease. [Washington, General, g. 5, p. 430]

List sources in the community where reliable information and advice on health questions may be obtained. Consider the dangers of self-prescribed patent medicines. [Idaho, General, g. 4-6, p. 223]

Topic 25. Household Preparations. Making or selecting soap, dye, paint, etc.
General: primary 4%; intermediate 11%. Social Studies: primary 13%; intermediate 9%.

The making of soap in a unit on colonial life is the only trace of this topic that can be found in most courses of study. In rare cases other household preparations may be made, or the selection of household preparations, especially soap, may be considered.

Make soap. Experiment with making different kinds by adding sand, kerosene, alcohol, etc. Collect samples of various builders used in soaps and samples of soaps used for various purposes. [Washington, General, g. 4, p. 542]

The making of soap is to help children understand some of the problems people must meet in making and distributing soap at such a reasonable cost. The purpose is not to develop an ability on the part of each child to make soap. [Los Angeles, Soc. Stu., g. 5, p. 261]

Are all washing powders, soaps, etc., of equal value? Is soft or hard water more satisfactory for cleaning purposes? What effect do borax, washing powder, and ammonia have upon hard water used in cleaning? Are flaky substances found in hard water containing a little soap visible when more soap is added? Can they all be dissolved? [Montana, Science, g. 4, pp. 5–7]

Collect and experiment with various types of cleansers. Have oral reports on the various cleaning activities that go on in the home. [Lakewood, Soc. Stu., g. 3, p. 43]

Mix some paint, using dry pigment and linseed oil. Demonstrate the preservative action of paint, oil, or varnish on samples of wood. Demonstrate the decorative value of various staining, varnishing, or polishing processes. (p. 72) Prepare dye from fruit juices, beets, onion skins, charcoal. (p. 63) [Denver, Soc. Stu., g. 4]

COMMENTS ON GROUP II, HOME LIFE IN OUR COMMUNITY

Six topics in this group occur much more frequently in the general courses than in the social studies courses. In the case of "Selecting a healthful diet," "Selecting clothing," "Care of clothing," and "Selection of remedies and treatments," the explanation is that these topics are most often found in outlines for health education, which are included in general but not in social studies courses. In the case of "Furnishing and interior decorating" and "Toys," above the primary levels these topics are most likely to appear in outlines for fine or industrial arts, which also are found in general but not in social studies courses.

Eight topics are much more common in primary grades than in intermediate grades. Three of these, "Planning and constructing a house," "Furnishing and decorating a house," and "Caring for and improving a house," occur in many courses only in connection with building, furnishing, and caring for a playhouse, an activity rarely found above second grade. That the topics "Actual preparation or preservation of foods" and "Serving Refreshments" are also much more frequent on the primary level than the intermediate is interesting. Can it be that the activity movement has not yet made great headway above the first three grades? That the topics taught chiefly by discussion—"Selecting clothing" and "Care of clothing"—are found in more primary than intermediate courses indicates that the consideration of these topics tends to be very elementary. In view of the importance of all eight of these topics and their undoubted interest to children, it seems unfortunate that they are not more often included in both primary and intermediate courses.

The low rank of "Toys: care, repair, making, selection" indicates neglect of one of the major interests of childhood and one of the most natural avenues for consumer education in the lower grades.

While "Care of clothing" is twentieth in rank among the fifty-six topics, "Household preparations" is thirty-seventh. This discrepancy gives further evidence that the instruction in care of clothing as outlined in most courses is superficial, omitting any attention to the selection of soap or other preparations used in laundering.

The most frequent topic in this group, "Selecting a healthful diet," occurs in 59 per cent of the general and social studies courses combined, or in 78 per cent of the general courses. Since consideration of the food value of even a single item of the diet was recorded as an occurrence of the topic, it is astonishing that the frequency is not closer to one hundred per cent.

Regarding the content of the topics, the following remarks may be of interest.

1. Ten of the topics in this group demand in the teacher a considerable knowledge of household science and household arts, and one requires a knowledge of nutrition. Without special training it appears unlikely that an elementary teacher can teach these topics so that all of their potential contribution to consumer education and the improvement of home life can be realized.

2. Very few of the courses indicate the specific knowledges and skills to be sought in the area of consumer education and household arts. In the absence of detailed guidance from the course of study, the teacher without special training in these areas is doubly handicapped.

3. The writers of most of the courses appear to have given insufficient thought to devising a content for this group of topics that will be likely to produce changes in behavior. Too much reliance is placed on talking about correct diet, suitable clothing, and healthful shelter, and too little attention is given to teaching ways by which families might obtain what

they need. To a fair proportion of courses, particularly those of the southeastern and south central states, this criticism does not apply.

4. It is a very rare course which indicates that any consideration is to be given to what constitutes the minimum acceptable standards for diet, clothing, and shelter of an American family. Only two instances can be cited, both concerning minimum standards in housing. (See excerpts on page 85 from the Missouri and the Fort Worth courses.) However, the State of Washington bulletin on social studies proposes study of a very significant problem designed to show the economy of providing the necessaries of life to everyone: "Is there a relation between an adequate supply of the basic needs (food, clothing, and shelter) and our value to the community?"[4]

GROUP III. CONSERVATION

Each of the three conservation topics occurs, on the average, in 119 courses, 28 per cent of the total. "Conservation of forests, flowers, and wild life" occurs in 52 per cent, ranking sixth in the entire list of topics. (See Table III, p. 100.)

Knowledge of conservation may be expected to increase one's economic competence by contributing to such understandings as these:

1. That the prosperity of our country is due in large measure to the abundance of our natural resources.

2. That many of our natural resources have already been so seriously depleted that we are now drawing on the supplies of other countries, which before long will also become scarce.

3. That the continuance of an industrial civilization is dependent upon an abundant supply of metals and fuels; therefore the utmost economy in their use is essential if our children's children are to enjoy the degree of prosperity we enjoy today.

4. That the continued destruction of our soil, like the destruction of other irreplaceable resources, is an economic loss which affects every individual.

5. That the renewal of those natural resources which are renewable

[4] Washington (State of), *An Integrated Social Science Curriculum for Elementary Grades*, p. 7. 1936.

may be expected to yield large returns both economically and in added enjoyment of the out-of-doors.

6. That the good citizen will do all he individually can to conserve natural resources, and will support government action for the same end.

Counting the Topics in Group III

This group involved no particular difficulties in counting. Any attention to the importance or the methods of conservation was counted, including discussion of ways to attract birds and the need to protect the scarcer kinds of wild flowers.

During the tabulating process the item "Conservation of property" was discarded, following the decision that this is an objective in all courses of study, whether or not it is expressed. The item "Conservation of human resources" was also discarded. It is found in a few courses, but its development is limited to the discussion of accident prevention. The concept of human life as an economic resource was not found in any course.

Materials from Courses of Study Illustrating the Content of Topics in Group III Likely to Contribute to Economic Competence

Topic 26. Conservation of Forests, Wild Flowers, and Animal Life. Helping wild birds; protecting wild flowers; learning about fish hatcheries, game preserves, and game laws.
General: primary 59%; intermediate 72%. Social Studies: primary 32%; intermediate 43%.

In the primary grades, this topic usually indicates the feeding of the winter birds and the listing of the wild flowers which need protection. In the intermediate grades, the economic importance of conservation may be developed, more often in connection with the forests than in connection with animal life.

CONSERVATION OF FORESTS

Our forests are being wasted. How does this affect you? How does it affect the next generation? What is the remedy? [Washington, General, g. 4–6, p. 404]

Tell how the destruction of forests raises the cost of living. Explain the saying, "Everybody loses when a forest burns." [Fort Worth, Soc. Stu., g. 5, pp. 92–3]

TABLE III

CONSERVATION

Topics Related to Economic Competence Found in General and Social Studies Courses

	COMBINED COURSES (420)		GENERAL COURSES (210)								SOCIAL STUDIES COURSES (210)							
			NUMBER AND PER CENT OF COURSES IN WHICH TOPIC APPEARS *															
			Grades								Grades							
TOPIC	No.	%	1	2	3	4	5	6	Total	%	1	2	3	4	5	6	Total	%
26. Forests, flowers, and wild life	217	52	19	21	22	25	26	25	138	66	11	8	15	10	22	13	79	38
27. Water control	74	18	0	0	2	3	7	10	22	10	0	1	3	22	14	12	52	25
28. Soil and minerals	66	16	0	0	15	4	9	10	38	18	0	0	3	4	13	8	28	13

* A course is the program for a single grade. For each grade 35 general courses and 35 social studies courses were tabulated.

Discuss measures to encourage reforestation: low taxes on land where timber is too young for cutting; cheap supplies of seed and seedlings; services of forest rangers and forest experiment stations. [Minnesota, General, g. 5, p. 504]

What kinds of lumber were cut from the ridges in the past and what varieties of trees are growing there now? (p. 93) What effect does the cutting off of forests have upon the brooks, water supplies, bird life, and soil fertility? How much money does the town pay for the support of schools? What would be the income from one hundred acres of pine forest if the piece were properly lumbered and replanted? Try to interest your selectmen in town forest planting. (p. 41) [Connecticut, Science, ungraded]

CONSERVATION OF BIRDS

Learning that birds help the farmer; that birds need help. Making bird-houses and feeding stations. [Brockton, Soc. Stu., g. 1, pp. 55–9]

What shrubs, trees, and plants carry fruit and seeds on which birds may feed in winter? Plant some about homes and school yards. (p. 58) In the spring put out various nesting materials; record the materials taken by different birds. (p. 63) [Connecticut, Science, ungraded]

Build a bird sanctuary on the school grounds or in your home yard. Plant shrubs, trees, vines, and flowers. Place birdhouses, feeding trays, and baths. Make your sanctuary as safe as possible from enemies of birds. [Amarillo, Science, g. 4, p. 4]

Making trips to observe bird conditions in the community. Making recommendations on the basis of these trips. [Glencoe, General, g. 5, p. 56]

CONSERVATION OF WILD FLOWERS

Making a picture listing of the flowers in the community that should never be picked. Making a collection of one of each type of flower that may be picked sparingly. Listing flowers that are becoming rare in our community. Making this information available to other children in the school. [Glencoe, General, g. 4, p. 50]

CONSERVATION OF WILD ANIMALS AND FISH

Making studies of the animal life of this section in frontier times and today. Listing wild animals that are of some economic value. [Glencoe, General, g. 4, p. 50]

Discuss the great variety of wild fowl, fish, and game animals in colonial days; their conservation today. [Fort Worth, Soc. Stu., g. 5, p. 50]

Discuss: fishing as a leisure-time activity, how fishing ranks as an industry in Wisconsin, how Wisconsin can promote fishing as a recreation industry. Interview: members of Conservation Department, commercial fishermen and dealers, sportsmen interested in fishing. Visit a fish hatchery. (Understandings sought: Fishing ranks as one of the nation's leading sports and in Wisconsin is a very important factor in the continuation of the recreation industry. By pollution of streams, by drainage of natural spawning grounds, and by damming power streams, men have destroyed many of the natural habitats of fish.) [Madison, Science, g. 5, pp. 14–7]

Topic 27. Water Control; Drainage, Irrigation, Flood Prevention. General: primary 2%; intermediate 19%. Social Studies: primary 4%; intermediate 48%.

Among the courses included in the count above, perhaps one-third indicate the study of some of the problems of water control in the United States; in the remainder the topic occurs only in the study of foreign countries, especially Egypt and The Netherlands.

Draw up plans for irrigating land, get pictures of irrigation projects. Is it profitable to irrigate land? [Amarillo, Science, g. 5, p. 2]

Make graphs to show how irrigation has increased the value of certain areas. Make maps showing irrigated regions of the United States. [Maryland, Science, g. 5, p. 158]

What are the different ways of irrigating land? What are the advantages and disadvantages of irrigation? Find pictures of the great irrigation dams built by the United States. Locate these on a map. Make a sand-table illustration of an irrigated area. Write a story telling of the changes which irrigation has made in any area studied. How and where has too much water proved a national problem? How has draining the land helped to add fertile farming areas? How do forests help to control droughts and floods? Where have terraced hillsides proved an answer to agricultural needs? [Binghamton, Soc. Stu., g. 6, *How Agriculture Supplies Man's Needs and Wants,* pp. 31–4]

Reading about and discussing what has been done to aid flood control in Arkansas. Visiting a dam, levee, or drainage ditch to observe what is being done to relieve flooded areas. Reporting on a federal flood control project in the State. Investigating to find out if flood control projects are being carried on in other countries. Reporting on what Holland has done to protect life and property from floods. Estimating the cost of flood control. Collecting and discussing statistical information on the loss of lives and property by floods. [Arkansas, General, g. 4–6, p. 149]

How can South Dakota conserve water for lakes and streams? What is the significance of our decreasing artesian well supply? What are the attitudes of various farm organizations on irrigation and drainage projects aided by the federal government? [South Dakota, Soc. Stu., g. 6, p. 776]

Topic 28. Conservation of Soil and Minerals.
General: primary 14%; intermediate 22%. Social Studies: primary 3%; intermediate 24%.

The topic "Soil conservation" occurs in over one-fifth of the intermediate courses tabulated. That soil erosion may be a problem in the local community which children can investigate is indicated in a small proportion of courses. Conservation of minerals is dealt with very much less frequently than conservation of soil.

SOIL DEPLETION AND EROSION; METHODS OF SOIL CONSERVATION

How do plants react to different kinds of soil? How do fertilizers affect the growth of plants? How do farmers keep the plant food in the soil from becoming exhausted? [Montgomery County, Science, g. 3, pp. 3–5]

Visit a place where running water has washed away some soil. Look at pictures of the Bad Lands, Grand Canyon, Hudson River, etc., and discuss the work of running water in changing the earth. Discuss the reasons for dust storms. Look at pictures of desert scenes showing sand dunes. Is dust and sand ever blown away by the wind where we live? What can we do to prevent this from happening? (g. 3, p. 52) Examine forest soil and compare it with soil found where few plants are growing. (g. 4, p. 166) Make a large map of the United States and indicate productive areas, mountainous areas, desert areas, and areas in which the soil is being blown or washed away. Compare the size of these areas. Look up figures on the number of acres under cultivation. On a large outline map of New York State indicate the areas of greatest productivity, the areas of worn-out land, and the areas of waste land. Collect pictures of eroded land areas. Observe places in your own vicinity where land has been destroyed by erosion. List the methods being tried to stop soil erosion and discuss the effectiveness of each. Has anything been done in your community in the interests of soil conservation? (g. 5, pp. 168–9) [New York, Science]

Write to the State Conservation Commission to ask what erosion is costing Tennessee per acre and what is the cost of preventive measures. (p. 79) Find out how many acres on your father's farm is losing its best soil by erosion. Find out what part of all the farms of the children in your grade is being lost by erosion. Estimate the cost of preventing erosion. Show pictures of how to plow or plant fields to help hold soil. Tell how you helped your father plant fields to hold soil. (p. 65) Discuss your plans for preventing erosion on the school ground. Organize your workers and outline the duties of each. (p. 79) [Hamilton County *Yearbook,* 1939–40, g. 5]

Bring samples of different types of soil to class and discuss each type as to its composition, appearance, and value for growing plants. What substances should be present in soil in order that it be favorable for growing plants? Collect and experiment with the different kinds of fertilizers sold in the stores. Report results. [Amarillo, Science, g. 6, pp. 3–4]

MINERALS: THEIR WASTE AND CONSERVATION

Nations which have advanced most are those which have made the largest use of minerals. (p. 75) Find out what can be done and is being done to conserve our minerals. Explain the phrase, "Mining, a robber industry." Discuss the importance of minerals to the industrial development of the world. (pp. 89–92) Discuss the probabilities of exhausting our coal and oil resources, and the necessity of conservation. Discuss possibilities of concentrating all our energy resources in the making of electric power. (p. 103) [Fort Worth, Soc. Stu., g. 5]

Look up the annual production of different mineral fuels and the estimated total deposits. Which are being used up most rapidly? How long will our supplies of important fuels last according to present estimates? Find examples of how fuels are being wasted. [New York, Science, g. 5, p. 170]

Essential learnings: The possession and use of vast amounts of coal is one of the chief causes for the comfortable way of living in the United States. A great proportion of the coal and oil supply of our country is wasted in mining, transporting, and burning. [Missouri, General, g. 5, p. 919]

Teacher should emphasize the facts: that when our minerals are gone there can be no replacing; that in the past a great deal has been wasted by taking out only the richer veins and leaving the poorer . . . and by allowing corporations to sell millions of dollars' worth of the choicest of our resources to foreign countries, therein benefiting themselves by deriving immense profits, but handicapping future generations. [Berkeley, Soc. Stu., g. 5, p. 316]

COMMENTS ON GROUP III, CONSERVATION

A generation has gone by since the calling of the first national conference on conservation by President Theodore Roosevelt. Meanwhile an unceasing campaign to make the American people aware of the urgent need for conservation has been carried on by private and public agencies. In response to this agitation, 66 per cent of the general courses tabulated are found to give some space to the topic "Conservation of forests, wild flowers, and wild life." Inasmuch as the outdoor world is so interesting to children, it is surprising that 34 per cent of the courses do not include any material on its conservation.

Water control and the conservation of soil and minerals are more important economically than conservation of living natural resources. But they are less interesting to young children, and probably for this reason are not so often presented on the primary level. So far as children's interests are concerned there seems to be no reason why these topics should not be taught in the intermediate grades in connection with the customary topics of farming, mining, and manufacturing. That so small a proportion of intermediate grade courses give attention either to water control or to the conservation of soil and minerals suggests that most course of study writers are very unclear on what information and understandings should be sought in the study of basic industries.

As to the content of the three conservation topics, the following comments may be made:

1. By far the most common conservation activities suggested have to do with attracting and protecting birds. This may be due to the fact that the National Audubon Society has been more active among teachers and school children than any other conservation agency.

2. The non-economic reasons for conservation of forests and wild life are stressed almost to the exclusion of the economic reasons. If our people are to think clearly on this subject they need to know the economic consequences of the destruction of these resources.

3. Above the primary level the suggested activities consist very largely of talking, reading, and writing about conservation. There is need of more attention to activities that involve observing and acting. (For examples see pp. 101–2 and p. 103)

GROUP IV. LOCAL COMMUNITY SERVICES AND THEIR SUPPORT

Each of the items in this group appears on the average in 86 courses, or 20 per cent of the total. (See Table IV, p. 106.)

The items deal with the common public services of the local com-

TABLE IV

LOCAL COMMUNITY SERVICES AND THEIR SUPPORT

Topics Related to Economic Competence Found in General and Social Studies Courses

NUMBER AND PER CENT OF COURSES IN WHICH TOPIC APPEARS *

TOPIC	COMBINED COURSES (420)		GENERAL COURSES (210)								SOCIAL STUDIES COURSES (210)							
	No.	%	Grades 1	2	3	4	5	6	Total	%	Grades 1	2	3	4	5	6	Total	%
29. Recreational facilities	131	31	9	19	12	6	8	7	61	29	14	22	17	6	7	4	70	33
30. Fire and police protection ..	126	30	15	14	9	9	6	4	57	27	20	23	13	5	4	4	69	33
31. Health protection	122	29	9	14	10	9	9	10	61	29	10	18	11	5	10	7	61	29
32. Water supply; sewage disposal	64	15	1	6	6	5	5	4	27	13	4	9	7	7	5	5	37	18
33. Public school system	39	9	0	2	1	6	7	3	19	9	2	4	2	4	4	4	20	10
34. Taxation	33	8	0	0	1	3	4	6	14	7	3	3	5	2	2	4	19	9

* A course is the program for a single grade. For each grade 35 general courses and 35 social studies courses were tabulated.

munity and how they are supported. Knowledge of these items may be expected to increase one's economic competence by:

1. Acquainting him with the variety of available services which he may sometime use.

2. Enabling him to compare the services available in his own community with those of other communities.

3. Preparing him to share in deciding whether the services offered should be extended, modified, or curtailed.

4. Acquainting him with the cost of the services and the essential facts about our system of taxation.

MATERIALS FROM COURSES OF STUDY ILLUSTRATING THE CONTENT OF TOPICS IN GROUP IV LIKELY TO CONTRIBUTE TO ECONOMIC COMPETENCE

Topic 29. Recreational Facilities Provided by the Community. General: primary 38%; intermediate 20%. Social Studies: primary 50%; intermediate 16%.

Typically this topic is designed to encourage children to use the public recreational facilities of the community, and suggests trips to such places as the public library, museums, parks, or zoological garden. In occasional courses some of the other implications for economic competence are developed.

Do you know who pays for and owns the parks and playgrounds? Tell ways you can help to keep these grounds clean and attractive. Desired outcomes: realization that city property costs money; that damage to it is a loss to every citizen. [St. Paul, Soc. Stu., g. 1, p. 39]

Visit the municipal recreation building, a park, museum, library, zoo. Make cooperative booklets showing how our community provides for recreation. Desired outcomes: (1) Understanding of: the value of play; what means of recreation are available and how to make the best use of them; (2) Appreciation of: the labor and expense involved in providing municipal recreation facilities; the work of the city recreation department; the taxpayer who provides the funds. [Fort Worth, Soc. Stu., g. 1, pp. 71–7]

Planning and building an outdoor oven. Such an activity may be the means of stimulating a feeling that not having but making is one's chief joy. [Mississippi, General, g. 2, p. 123]

Explain the value of a community recreation center. Prepare some playground equipment. [Missouri, General, g. 6, pp. 953–4]

Determine what recreation is and discuss necessity for different types. Plan and build a model community showing swimming pool, parks, playgrounds, community building, golf course, etc. Make a graph showing the recreational facilities of the county and the number of people using them. Select a vacant lot in the community and prepare plans for making it useful and attractive. [Texas, General, g. 6, pp. 77–8]

If the people of the city may expect to have shorter hours of work in future, what can the community do to offer better opportunities for wholesome recreation? [Houston, Soc. Stu., high g. 6, unit 3, p. 27]

Topic 30. The Fire Department; the Police Department.
General: primary 36%; intermediate 18%. Social Studies: primary 53%; intermediate 12%.

The economic aspects of this very common topic are seldom indicated. Furthermore, the work of the police department, beyond the control of traffic, is seldom treated. The materials below do not, therefore, represent typical materials for the development of this topic.

THE FIRE DEPARTMENT

Discuss qualifications necessary for a fireman. Discuss the duties and work of a fireman. Who pays the firemen for their work? [Iowa, History, g. 1–2, p. 23]

Find out: cost of equipment of firemen; number of firemen and their salaries; comparison with salaries in other positions. [Muskogee, Arithmetic, g. 4, p. 142]

Determine the average annual fire loss in Fort Worth and compare with that in other cities. Find out how Fort Worth's fire insurance rates compare with those in other Texas cities. Determine how much Fort Worth spends each year for fire prevention. How many firemen are employed? What are their salaries? What is the cost of fire trucks and other equipment? [Fort Worth, Arithmetic, g. 6, p. 311]

THE POLICE DEPARTMENT

Visit police station. Interview police captain, police woman, traffic officer, detectives. Discuss: organization of the police department, the police signal system, finger printing, how police are chosen. [Lakewood, Soc. Stu., g. 1, p. 41]

Interviewing a local officer or detective about his work. Finding how policemen prevent crimes as well as apprehend lawbreakers. [Arkansas, General, g. 4–6, p. 142]

Topic 31. Health Protection. The health department. What nurses, doctors, clinics, and hospitals do; safeguards provided by the community to insure pure food and drugs; cost of ill-health.

General: primary 31%; intermediate 27%. Social Studies: primary 37%; intermediate 21%.

The principal aims of this common topic seem to be to win the willing cooperation of the pupils with the health department and to acquaint them with the available health services of the community. The economic implications of the topic are not often developed.

Discuss how the community protects our health: (1) by keeping the city clean; (2) by quarantine; (3) by providing hospitals to care for the sick; (4) by employing people to help care for our health. [California, Soc. Stu., g. 3, p. 45]

Visit a clinic to see measures used in preventing and controlling disease. Collect data showing how governmental control has decreased the death rate from typhoid, diphtheria, and smallpox. [Arkansas, General, g. 4–6, pp. 134–5]

List the agencies in your community that protect your health. Find out what each agency does. Examine labels and stamps indicating that food and drugs have undergone inspection. Find out about the Pure Food and Drugs Act. Have some member of the class tell about the inspection of grocery stores, delicatessens, restaurants, and meat markets. [New York, Science, g. 6, p. 174]

How does the community protect against impure food and drugs? Care for those who are sick and cannot afford medical treatment? Care for the health of its school children? Prevent the spread of communicable diseases? [Houston, *Science Units for High Sixth Grade*, pp. 43–4. Not tabulated]

What is the cost of disease to the individual? To the community? Why has New York City built so many hospitals in various parts of New York State? How has this helped build up the state? [Ossining, N. Y., *Our Community and Westchester County*, g. 4, pp. 9–10. Not tabulated]

How could our health be improved through more adequate medical care? List public health facilities of your community. Compare your community with another community as to health services provided. [Texas, *Tentative Course of Study, Grades One to Six*, g. 6, p. 211. Not tabulated]

Discuss the economic value of the City Health Department. [Fort Worth, Arithmetic, g. 4, p. 137]

Topic 32. Water Supply; Sewage Disposal.
General: primary 12%; intermediate 13%. Social Studies: primary 19%; intermediate 16%.

Typically this topic deals with the community water system rather than the water supply of rural homes. The sub-topic, sewage disposal, is rare.

Discuss various ways of getting water. Discuss why city people must pay for the water they use; why people in the country do not pay for the water they use. [Iowa, Geography, g. 1, p. 46]

Investigate the school well with regard to location, cover, filter, and construction. Send a specimen of the water to the State Department of Public Health for testing. Investigate the water supply of individual homes, letting each individual make a sketch of the well, barn, and outbuildings of his own home. [Illinois, Science, g. 4–6, p. 28]

Visit the waterworks to find out: Where does your city or town get its water? How is the water made pure and safe? How many gallons of water does each person use daily? How much does water cost per gallon? Make a model filter using layers of sand, charcoal, and gravel in a glass chimney. [Iowa, Science, g. 4–6, p. 84]

Unit: "How We Secure a Water Supply for Our Homes." Outline of content: Water supply (1) in a farmhouse—meaning of a well, how water is pumped into storage tanks, how it is safeguarded from contamination, how made available as running water in a farmhouse; (2) in a city home—meaning of city reservoirs, source of water supply, how water in reservoirs is purified, function of city water-pumping stations, purpose of city mains. [Denver, Soc. Stu., g. 4, p. 69]

Topic 33. The Public School System of the Community.
General: primary 3%; intermediate 15%. Social Studies: primary 8%; intermediate 11%.

The informal study of the pupils' own school, so common in the primary grades, was not counted unless consideration of how schools are supported and controlled or of the school system as a whole was indicated.

How are public schools controlled and supported? Why do we establish free public schools? Do country boys and girls have the same educational advantages as city boys and girls? When you are absent from school for a day, how much does your district lose? What do you lose? [Washington, General, g. 4–6, p. 395]

Find out how many cents of every tax dollar go for schools. Why are public schools cheaper than private schools? Why does the state want boys and girls to have an education? Discuss our responsibility for the proper care of books, desks, and other school equipment. Plan a program for Education Week portraying all the educative agencies of Fort Worth. Write a guidebook for Fort Worth, pointing out all the educational institutions. [Fort Worth, Soc. Stu., g. 4, pp. 168–80]

Find cost of schooling per pupil to the city. Compare cost in primary grades, intermediate grades, and high school. Compare cost in Muskogee with cost in other cities. [Muskogee, Arithmetic, g. 5, p. 161]

Find cost of building and maintaining our school buildings. Find cost of education per capita in Baltimore. Compare it with that of other cities. [Baltimore, Arithmetic (1929), g. 6, p. 112]

Find approximate cost for a month's supplies for one pupil; for the grade. Seek cooperation in reducing cost of supplies for one month by economy in their use. Compute saving for the grade, for the entire school. [New York, Arithmetic, g. 5, p. 79]

Discuss: Why should citizens who have no children in Houston's schools be expected to pay taxes for the upkeep of the schools? [Houston, Soc. Stu., high g. 6, unit 3, p. 58]

Finding out how the school board buys supplies; how they give all companies a fair chance to offer their wares. [Houston, Soc. Stu., low g. 6, unit 2, p. 11]

Topic 34. Taxation. Who pays taxes; kinds of taxes; how taxes are expended; government borrowing.
General: primary 1%; intermediate 12%. Social Studies: primary 10%; intermediate 8%.

While taxation has passing mention in many courses, the number which consider the processes and kinds of taxation or the way the tax money is apportioned are few, as the figures above demonstrate.

Find out who pays taxes. Who pays for the school building, coal, and teachers' salaries? What part of a person's taxes are for the school? Who is the loser when pupils damage school property? Find out how much tax was paid on certain farms fifty years ago, forty years ago, thirty, twenty, and ten years ago. [Kansas, Soc. Stu., g. 3, pp. 94–5]

Consult your parents' tax receipts on real and personal property taxes. Find out what part of the taxes went for the support of the school district, the town, the city, the county, and the state government. Visit your county seat; study the county buildings and the uses made of each; find out the cost of county buildings, land, bridges, culverts, roads, and parks. How was the money secured? Find the amount of revenue required to support services of the state government. How much is used for education? for highways? List the ways in which you are directly benefited by state expenditures. [Washington, General, g. 4–6, p. 398]

Discuss: Why taxes are necessary; people who pay taxes, work of the assessors and tax collector. [New Hampshire, General, g. 4–5, p. 455]

Should the farmer be taxed for the good road that passes his farm? Why? [Detroit, Soc. Stu., g. 6, p. 279]

Report how money is provided for carrying on the affairs of the national, state, and city government. Make a chart telling how one tax dollar is used. Prepare short dramatizations showing how taxes are levied, how they are collected, how they are used. (high g. 6, unit 1, p. 23) Upon what are taxes levied? Are there differences of opinion among taxpayers as to how taxes should be raised? (high g. 6, unit 3, p. 58) [Houston, Soc. Stu.]

Visit City Hall, the Court House, and other municipal offices. Study the city budget. Make graphs showing in per cents the relative amounts spent for various departments. Discuss cost of construction and maintenance of sewers. Discuss General Improvement Loan and Municipal Bonds (interpretative knowledge only). Calculate interest on municipal bonds. [Baltimore, Arithmetic (1929), g. 6, p. 116]

COMMENTS ON GROUP IV

Three topics in this group, "Community recreational facilities," "Fire and police protection," and "Health protection," tend to occur together in a unit, "Our Community," found in many primary and some intermediate courses. The other three topics occur only one-half to one-fourth as often. It is somewhat surprising that the public school system ranks no higher, for the subject is no more difficult than the others in this group, and is surely no less important. It is a topic that should be of considerable interest to children.

As to the content of the topics in the courses analyzed, there is a striking difference between the poorest and the best examples. In the poorer, the treatment is purely descriptive. In the better, such economic implications may be brought out as the cost of the services, their economic value to the community, their proportionate share in the community budget, the salaries paid to the officials and other employees, how money was raised through bond issues for the buildings, and how money is raised through taxation for their operation.

GROUP V. CHARACTERISTICS OF A MACHINE CIVILIZATION

The twelve topics of this group appear on the average in 63 courses each (15 per cent) of the 420 general and social studies courses. One item, "Interdependence," is fourth in rank among the entire list. Eight topics fall below the median, and seven fall in the lowest quarter. The group as a whole ranks fifth in average frequency of topics. The importance of the ideas involved is greater than the frequency of their appearance would signify. (See Table V, p. 114.)

The items deal with various characteristics of a machine civilization, such as mass production and world trade, and some of its typical problems, such as unemployment. Study of these matters may contribute to economic competence to the extent that it develops:

1. Appreciation of economic interdependence and its practical consequences.
2. Awareness of the social-economic problems of our society.
3. Realization that these problems are not due to the ill will of some small group but to economic customs, traditions, and laws which are not suited to modern conditions.
4. Understanding of the need for the organization of labor.
5. Appreciation of the waste represented by unemployment and unused industrial plants.
6. Awareness that this country has the natural resources, capital, labor, and managerial skill to attain an adequate standard of living for all.
7. An interest in world trade and its relation to world peace and prosperity.

These learnings concern the great issues of our time. Undoubtedly they can and should begin in the elementary school.

Counting the Topics in Group V

More difficulty was experienced in defining the topics in this group than in others, but after some initial fumbling, nearly all the items that could be looked for became clear.

TABLE V

CHARACTERISTICS OF A MACHINE CIVILIZATION

Topics Related to Economic Competence Found in General and Social Studies Courses

NUMBER AND PER CENT OF COURSES IN WHICH TOPIC APPEARS*

TOPIC	COMBINED COURSES (420)		GENERAL COURSES (210)								SOCIAL STUDIES COURSES (210)							
	No.	%	Grades 1	2	3	4	5	6	Total	%	Grades 1	2	3	4	5	6	Total	%
35. Interdependence	233	55	6	15	15	16	17	19	88	42	26	26	25	16	22	30	145	69
36. Trade; markets	132	31	0	6	10	10	15	14	55	26	3	8	11	17	17	21	77	37
37. World trade; tariffs	131	31	0	0	4	10	12	23	49	23	0	1	15	16	22	28	82	39
38. Machines: how changed ways of living	95	23	0	0	3	2	19	11	35	17	0	4	5	11	20	20	60	29
39. Standards of living: comparative	48	11	0	0	1	2	5	8	16	7	0	0	4	6	10	12	32	15
40. Labor conditions and problems	40	10	0	0	0	5	5	5	15	7	0	0	2	3	10	10	25	12
41. Mass production; specialization	29	7	0	0	0	1	5	8	14	7	0	1	4	3	3	4	15	7
42. Unemployment	16	4	0	0	0	1	1	2	4	2	1	0	0	0	4	7	12	6
43. Growth of big business; regulation of business	12	3	0	0	0	0	2	3	5	2	0	0	0	2	2	3	7	3
44. Labor organization; strikes; lockouts	11	3	0	0	0	0	1	1	2	1	0	0	0	1	4	4	9	4
45. Distribution of income; concentration of wealth	7	2	0	0	0	0	1	2	3	1	0	0	0	1	1	2	4	2
46. Prospects of attaining an adequate standard of living	4	1	0	0	0	1	1	2	4	2	0	0	0	0	0	0	0	0

* A course is the program for a single grade. For each grade 35 general courses and 35 social studies courses were tabulated.

As in tabulating other groups of topics, search was made for ideas and not for any particular verbal formulas. The original topic of "Industrial Revolution" was retitled "How machines have changed our ways of living" when it became apparent that this is a truer description of the content subsumed under this heading in elementary courses. The ideas of mass production, specialization, and standard of living were counted whether or not so named, insofar as they could be positively identified.

The topic "Population problems and movements" was discarded at the end of the tabulating process. Although it appears occasionally in geography outlines for fifth and sixth grades, its real economic implications are not brought out. The economic generalization most often associated with it—that a low standard of living is due to overpopulation—is a gross oversimplification. For this reason, the topic was not included in the final list.

Throughout the tabulating process the broad heading "Capitalism" was retained, in case any materials should be found dealing with the nature of capitalism as distinguished from other economic systems. In the end it was found that the materials gathered could be more accurately described by a new heading, "Distribution of income; concentration of wealth," and accordingly this was substituted.

MATERIALS FROM COURSES OF STUDY ILLUSTRATING THE CONTENT OF TOPICS IN GROUP V LIKELY TO CONTRIBUTE TO ECONOMIC COMPETENCE

Topic 35. Interdependence of Individuals, Communities, Regions, and Nations.
General: primary 34%; intermediate 50%. Social Studies: primary 73%; intermediate 65%.

Of the topics tabulated this is the second most frequent in social studies courses and the tenth most frequent in general courses. The typical development of the topic is designed to make plain that individuals, communities, and regions are interdependent. Less often the interdependence of nations is indicated. The consequences of interdependence are not often brought out.

List the community helpers who supply our community needs for food, clothing, and shelter. (g. 1, p. 33) Build a miniature community in which may be dramatized the daily contacts between a family and the community helpers. Make a cooperative booklet showing how dependent the family is upon community helpers for their assistance in securing food, clothing, and shelter. (g. 1, p. 35) Make pictures showing how many people have helped to make a handkerchief, a sweater, a hat, etc. (g. 4, p. 160) [Fort Worth, Soc. Stu.]

To aid in building concepts of interdependence, plan and carry out a pageant or play; let people from foreign lands tell what food products are sent to the United States; have the farmer, fisherman, cowboy, baker, miller, salt miner, railroad worker, grocer, etc., each tell his part in satisfying man's need for food. (g. 4, p. 57) To aid in building concepts of interdependence among industries, use charts to show industries dependent on iron and steel; industries dependent upon raw materials from farms, fisheries, forests, grazing lands, mines, or quarries. (g. 6, p. 141) [Denver, Soc. Stu.]

Discuss and find reasons for the interdependence of the East and the West. [Binghamton, Soc. Stu., g. 5, *Life and Work in the Great West,* p. 17]

Make a report to show that a depression in one country affects the welfare of many countries. [Houston, Soc. Stu., high g. 6, unit 1, p. 38]

How does man's increasing control over nature make people and groups more interdependent? [Malverne, Soc. Stu., g. 3, p. 1. Not-tabulated.]

Suggested Principles: All over the world people are contributing in some way toward the things we use, eat, or wear each day. (g. 3, p. 23) People in different localities have different advantages which make exchange and cooperation necessary. (g. 4, p. 24) No nation can economically or socially depend upon itself. (g. 5, p. 25) Regions possessing abundance of certain resources tend to develop these resources and depend upon other regions for other necessaries. (g. 5, p. 26) [Berkeley, Soc. Stu.]

Topic 36. Trade. History of trade; development of the use of money; meaning of "market"; meaning of "hinterland"; how prices are established; stock and commodity exchanges.
General: primary 15%; intermediate 37%. Social Studies: primary 21%; intermediate 53%.

In most courses this topic is concerned chiefly with the picturesque features of ancient and medieval trade, or with the evolution of a metallic medium of exchange. The factors that help or hinder trade, the factors that influence prices, the concept of a hinterland, or the functions of stock and commodity exchanges are mentioned in a small proportion of courses.

THE HISTORY OF TRADE

Finding the methods of exchange used by primitive peoples; using the monies of these peoples; finding what things are traded with the Eskimos and other frontier peoples. (g. 3, pp. 42–3) Preparing an exhibit showing articles that brought about trade in Crusade times. (g. 4, p. 52) Organizing a group on the guild basis and planning a fair of materials made by the handicraft methods of medieval times; comparing the trade methods of the present day with those of feudal days. (g. 5, pp. 52–4) [Glencoe, General]

Comparing how food was purchased in pioneer days with how it is purchased today. Comparing costs. [Long Beach, Arithmetic, g. 4, p. 24]

DEVELOPMENT OF THE USE OF MONEY

Reading to discover that men have not always used money, and why metal finally came into use as the medium of exchange. Discussing why people are willing to accept paper money. [Mississippi, General, g. 6, pp. 282–3]

Prepare a report explaining the meaning and use of token money. Explain how paper money derives its value. Bring to class some Confederate money. Why can we not buy things with Confederate money today? [Houston, Soc. Stu., g. 6, p. 23]

Do the pupils understand the meaning of money, the gold standard, paper money? [Maryland, Soc. Stu., g. 4–6, p. 141]

MEANING OF TERMS "MARKET" AND "HINTERLAND"

Locate on an outline map five or six of the most important markets for farm products. [Indiana, Soc. Stu., g. 6, p. 134]

Find out what is meant by a hinterland. Show how transportation facilities influence the growth of a hinterland. (g. 5, p. 115) Build two miniature freight trains, one loaded with raw materials from our hinterland, the other ready to distribute Fort Worth products to the rest of the world. On an outline map of Texas mark Fort Worth's trade territory and show the products in pictorial form. (g. 6, p. 57) [Fort Worth, Soc. Stu.]

FACTORS THAT HELP OR HINDER TRADE

Discuss the subject of markets for Texas products, naming the conditions that may lead to a greater demand for Texas products in the future. [Fort Worth, Soc. Stu., g. 6, p. 93]

How the credit plan of buying has increased trade. How trade is encouraged because there is no tariff on goods shipped within the United States. [Oklahoma City, Soc. Stu., g. 5, p. 106]

What effect did tolls have on trade during the Middle Ages? [Minneapolis, Arithmetic, g. 6, p. 97]

Understandings to be developed: Communication and ease of transportation increase the output of trade products. Distance from available markets determines whether a region will raise products for trade or home consumption. The value of farms is influenced by the distance from a market for their products. [Berkeley, Soc. Stu., g. 5, pp. 26–7]

Commercial activities depend upon world peace. [Fort Worth, Soc. Stu., g. 5, p. 28]

HOW PRICES ARE ESTABLISHED; FUNCTION OF STOCK AND COMMODITY EXCHANGES

Find out what kind of business is carried on at a cotton exchange. Why is it important to have stock exchanges and cotton exchanges? Find out how the price of cotton is determined. Dramatize a scene in the cotton exchange showing how a man in San Francisco might buy cotton grown in Texas from a man in New York. [Houston, Soc. Stu., g. 5, unit 4, pp. 11–3]

Comparing the buying and selling of cotton on a modern cotton exchange and in the early history of the United States. Picturing on a map the cotton markets of the world. [Los Angeles County, General, g. 5, p. 205]

Observing the unloading of perishable cargo; estimating the cost of delay in unloading; gaining acquaintance with how inspectors check on basis of "law of averages"; getting insight into how retail price is established. [Long Beach, Arithmetic, g. 6, p. 28]

Generalizations that may be developed: Prices vary with the cost of production. A dominating factor in determining prices is the competition of the market. [Fort Worth, Soc. Stu., g. 6, p. 88]

Topic 37. World Trade; Tariffs.
General: primary 4%; intermediate 43%. Social Studies: primary 15%; intermediate 63%.

The first sample given below is typical of the content of this topic. The samples which deal with the conditions favoring or hampering world trade and which suggest that a nation to sell abroad must buy abroad are superior to what can be found in most courses. Tariffs are considered in a small proportion of the courses that include world trade; consideration of the arguments against protective tariffs is seldom indicated.

Make posters showing what the United States buys from each country of Europe; what they buy from the United States. [Michigan, General, g. 6, p. 133] Study trade maps and tables and make graphs showing the amount and kinds of trade between the United States and Australia.

THE RECIPROCAL NATURE OF WORLD TRADE

How does Belgium pay for imports of food? Why are Denmark's colonies of less value to her than the Dutch colonies are to the Netherlands? What conditions enable a country to become a trading nation? [Utah, Soc. Stu., g. 6, pp. 25–8]

Discuss the reason why Holland, without enough land to feed herself, devotes good grain fields to the growth of flowering bulbs. Discuss the dependence of the Swiss upon their neighbors. Desired outcome: appreciation of the economic relationships between the countries of the world. [Fort Worth, Soc. Stu., g. 4, pp. 131–2]

What does England take from Argentina in return for its coal? Is it important that we buy from other countries as well as sell to them? [Houston, Soc. Stu., low g. 6, unit 1, p. 15]

Are there any parts of the world that could use our surplus of cotton and wheat? Why do we sometimes have difficulty in selling these products? (Other countries cannot buy our products unless they have products which we will buy from them. Edr.) [Houston, Soc. Stu., low g. 6, unit 3, p. 8]

REASONS FOR IMPORTING CERTAIN COMMODITIES

See if you can find any crop reports and prices quoted from Argentina. Find out why the United States trades with Argentina when both have the same products. [Iowa, Geography, g. 5, pp. 131–2]

Find out why the United States does not grow more tea. [Fort Worth, Soc. Stu., g. 3, pp. 252]

Bring to class articles stamped "Made in Japan." Discuss how these differ in workmanship and price from products made in the United States and reasons for the difference. . . . Make a list of goods which Russia buys from us and which she sells to us and discuss reasons for the difference in kind. [Binghamton, Soc. Stu., g. 6, *How Manufacturing Supplies Our Needs and Wants*, pp. 30–1]

TARIFFS

What is a tariff and why necessary? What is free trade? What has been the attitude of the South toward a high protective tariff? What are the advantages of a high protective tariff? [Missouri, General, g. 6, p. 791]

Can you think of any reason why the United States should put a tariff on goods manufactured from cotton? Which section of the country would benefit from the tariff on cotton goods, the manufacturing centers or the agricultural centers? Why? Find out whether your father believes in a high or low tariff or none at all, and his reasons. Tell the class. [Houston, Soc. Stu., g. 5, unit 4, p. 14]

Topic 38. How Machines Have Changed Our Ways of Living; the Industrial Revolution.

General: primary 3%; intermediate 30%. Social Studies: primary 9%; intermediate 49%.

Typically this topic considers the conveniences and luxuries that machines have given us without going into the social-economic consequences of the use of machinery.

HOW PRODUCTIVE AND TRADING METHODS HAVE BEEN CHANGED

Reading about and reporting the development of the factory system of producing goods. Discussing the physiological differences between hand and machine labor. Dyeing cloth by primitive and commercial methods and comparing the results. Making hand looms and weaving rugs to demonstrate changes that have been brought about by the machine. Investigating how machinery has revolutionized the rubber industry. Surveying the community to find the influence of the machine upon its trade. [Arkansas, General, intermediate grades, p. 167]

Work out illustrations of the distributive and productive systems of the feudal period in comparison with the modern agencies serving Glencoe. Visiting present large industrial organizations and comparing method and product with those of the skilled artisan of the feudal period. [Glencoe, General, g. 5, pp. 52–3]

SOCIAL-ECONOMIC CONSEQUENCES OF THE INDUSTRIAL REVOLUTION

Explain how the invention of the sewing machine affected the clothing industry. Discuss the number of people employed in the making of clothing who would not be so employed if the making of clothing had not been transferred to the factory. (g. 4, pp. 115–6) Find out if the use of machinery reduces the cost of labor. Make a bar graph comparing the length of the average work day now, during your grandfather's time, and during pioneer days. List the machines that replace man labor and show how the number of factory workers has been reduced. (g. 5, pp. 202–3) [Fort Worth, Arithmetic]

Develop an understanding of conditions that arose when people became machine tenders, paid by wages instead of selling their own produce. (Large cities, slums, neglect of children because both parents employed at low wages.) [Berkeley, Soc. Stu., g. 5, p. 304]

Place pictures on the board that show the activities of keeping house before and after labor-saving devices were invented. [Amarillo, Science, g. 6, p. 3]

Working out plays or stories to show what our community would be without the inventions that make our type of life possible. (g. 4, p. 46) Listing ways in which labor-saving devices have contributed to increased leisure. (g. 5, p. 53) [Glencoe, General]

Make a list of the things we have today which were unknown to great-grandmother. List the industries of Fort Worth. Have Americans always been engaged in these industries? (g. 5, p. 47) Find out how the introduction of machines changed independent workers to dependent wage earners. Find out how the Industrial Revolution brought growth of population, wealth, and prosperity to England. (g. 6, p. 117) [Fort Worth, Soc. Stu.]

Topic 39. Comparative Standards of Living: Of classes or areas, or of peoples of different periods. Reasons for low or high standards of living.

General: primary 1%; intermediate 14%. Social Studies: primary 4%; intermediate 27%.

Usually this topic indicates that our standards of living are higher than those of other countries, and higher today than in former times. A few courses give reasons for the differences, but there are not many suggestions as to how to make the reasons clear to children.

DIFFERENCES OF LIVING STANDARDS IN VARIOUS PLACES AND PERIODS

Read to find out how tea pickers dress and what they eat. How much are they paid? How do they live on their wages? [Fort Worth, Soc. Stu., g. 3, pp. 252-5]

Contrast the standards of living of Mexicans and Texans. Compare the Mexican's idea of the necessaries of life with the American's. Why have the American standards of living advanced more rapidly than the Mexican standards? [Fort Worth, Arithmetic, g. 6, p. 254]

Compare standards of living in Houston today with those in a community of long ago. [Houston, Soc. Stu., high g. 6, unit 1, p. 30]

Plan short sketches comparing the relative standards of living of different periods of the world's history. [Glencoe, General, g. 5, p. 55]

REASONS FOR LOW OR HIGH STANDARDS OF LIVING

Generalizations to develop: The utilization of natural resources is important in determining the wealth or poverty of a people. (p. 75) Increased trade and transportation tend to improve standards of living. (p. 28) [Fort Worth, Soc. Stu., g. 5]

Generalization to develop: man's understanding and control of electricity have revolutionized living standards in a single generation. [Madison, Science, g. 6, p. 24]

Understandings to be sought: machines and quantity production provide us with many luxuries. Science and invention are directly responsible for higher standards of living and the opportunities for leisure and cultural pursuits. Intended outcome: respect for man's ability to raise the standards of living through his power to invent. [Amarillo, Science, g. 6, pp. 1–2]

Why is China with its great area and mineral wealth not a prosperous nation today? How can China (proper) with less than two-thirds of the area of the United States support four times as many people? What industries are being developed that will help support the people? [Nevada, General, g. 6, p. 182]

Topic 40. Labor Conditions and Problems. Occupational hazards and diseases, working conditions, hours of work, child labor, labor legislation, the problems of low wages and cheap labor.
General: primary 0%; intermediate 14%. Social Studies: primary 2%; intermediate 22%.

Typically this topic deals with the prevention of industrial accidents, with legislation to improve working conditions, and with the provisions made by enlightened employers for the comfort, health, and safety of their workers.

WORKING CONDITIONS AND HAZARDS; LABOR LEGISLATION

Show slides picturing the life of lumbermen, fishermen, and miners. Discuss the hardships and dangers of their work. [Fort Worth, Soc. Stu., g. 5, pp. 86–7]

Discuss hazards in mining and methods of elimination. Read about and discuss health and accident conditions among factory workers. Read about and discuss "sweat shops," where they are located, who works in them, how they affect the lives of workers and the price of commodities they manufacture. [Virginia, General, g. 6, pp. 184–9]

Is there a factory for making cloth or clothing in the town? Find out how many hours a day the employees work. Find out how the building is lighted, heated, and ventilated. How might the employer improve working conditions for the employee? What regulations does the city make for the comfort of factory employees? [Minnesota, General, g. 4, p. 357]

Look up the Texas labor laws. What is said about minimum wages, hours of work, overtime work, child labor and age restrictions, safety appliances, etc.? [Fort Worth, Arithmetic, g. 6, p. 273]

Find out whether or not children are employed in Houston mills. Read articles about child labor in southern mills. Is this condition improving or not? [Houston, Soc. Stu., g. 5, unit 4, p. 44]

Make a list of occupational diseases and find the conditions conducive to them. Compare working conditions in factories of other countries with those of the United States. Investigate the conditions under which prisoners of the state work. [Texas, General, g. 5, p. 62]

WAGES

Find out why the workers can afford to work for lower wages in the South than in New England. (p. 106) Explain why human labor is so cheap in Egypt. Compare wages paid for labor in Egypt with wages paid for labor in Texas. (p. 88) Explain the relation of cheap human labor to the silk industry. (p. 110) [Fort Worth, Arithmetic, g. 4]

Why is labor so much cheaper in China than in the United States? (g. 5, p. 175) All of us that work, work for a wage. What is a just or reasonable wage? (g. 6, p. 272) [Detroit, Soc. Stu.]

Topic 41. Mass Production; Specialization.
General: primary 0%; intermediate 13%. Social Studies: primary 5%; intermediate 10%.

In most cases this topic indicates what is meant by mass production and specialization by contrasting production methods in a modern factory with those used by craftsmen long ago. The potentialities of mass production for raising the standard of living are sometimes mentioned. The problem of so-called over-production is mentioned in two courses.

Contrast the way in which your great-grandfather's shoes were made with the way in which yours are made today by discussing the following points: materials used, amount of time, division of labor, labor cost. [Fort Worth, Arithmetic, g. 4, p. 112]

Discussing reasons for the increased quantities and the standardized colors and patterns of glassware. [Arkansas, General, g. 4–6, p. 168]

Reporting on why standardized goods are cheaper than handmade goods. Comparing the cost of home and commercial products and services. Visiting an industrial plant to see how rapidly and cheaply articles for home consumption can be produced [Virginia, General, g. 6, p. 193]

In a broad way children should gain an understanding of the social and economic results of mass production. They should gain an understanding of the possibilities of a higher standard of living due to the production of the necessaries of life on the scale now practiced and that to be expected in the future. [Mississippi, General, g. 6, p. 250]

What may happen if the physical environment is so favorable that a people produce more than they can use? Does over-production necessarily bring good times to the whole nation? If it were possible to have equal distribution of products to all the people who need them, would it be possible to have over-production? [Houston, Soc. Stu., low g. 6, unit 3, p. 8]

What are the economic results of over-production? [Minneapolis, Arithmetic, g. 6, p. 97]

Topic 42. Unemployment, Its Causes, and Methods of Dealing with It.
General: primary 0%; intermediate 4%. Social Studies: primary 1%; intermediate 10%.

In few courses in which this topic occurs are there any definite suggestions for its development. The following are the best examples.

Visiting the local relief office for information about services rendered the unemployed. Investigating and reporting on home conditions of the unemployed. Investigating how the housing program is helping the unemployed. Reading about and discussing how shorter working hours have distributed work and helped unemployment. Visiting a rural rehabilitation project to observe how unemployed persons are given employment. Reading to find out how other countries care for their unemployed. Discussing the kind of relief that is best for the unemployed. [Arkansas, General, g. 4–6, p. 141]

Discuss: If a man can't get work in the city today, why doesn't he go to the country and take a farm of his own? What does land around Houston cost today? Some land in western Texas is very cheap; why does it not attract farmers to it in large numbers? Why is it that the smaller number of persons living on farms today can produce all that is needed to supply the demand for farm products? Is the increasing scarcity of desirable land the only thing that is tending to produce unemployment and lower wages? If a new frontier were opened today would it attract great numbers of people? Since we no longer have a frontier and competition is likely to become even more keen, what can boys and girls do to prepare themselves to make a living? [Houston, Soc. Stu., g. 5, unit 3, p. 3]

Do we find from history that the United States has had many business depressions or panics? What are some of the causes that lead to business depressions? Is there any way by which business firms could help to decrease the amount of unemployment (in a depression)? What are some of the suggestions offered by writers and radio speakers for averting depressions? [Houston, Soc. Stu., high g. 6, unit 1, p. 5]

Discuss the displacement of labor by machines as shown by unemployment. (p. 100) Get material for a report on automatic machines and their influence on present-day labor conditions. (p. 103) Prepare a report on the unemployment problems of Great Britain. (p. 119) [Fort Worth, Soc. Stu., g. 6]

Unit title suggested for year six: "Investigating the Problem of Our Country's Resources and Equipment in Fulfilling Our Need for Employment." [Texas, General, g. 6, p. 86] Also cited on p. 128.

Topic 43. The Growth of Big Business. Regulation of the public utility companies; problems associated with the rise of big business.

General: primary 0%; intermediate 5%. Social Studies: primary 0%; intermediate 7%.

Only three of the courses tabulated contained any mention of efforts or agencies to regulate businesses engaged in providing public utilities. Although a few courses contain generalizations regarding some of the problems associated with the rise of big business, these courses do not show how the generalizations are to be developed in the classroom.

THE GROWTH OF BIG BUSINESS

Find out about the evolution of some large corporation whose business it is to provide means of transportation. [Missouri, General, g. 5, p. 929]

How have our great corporations developed? (p. 25) List some of the very large corporations of the United States. Report to the class on how the large corporation makes mass production possible. (p. 30) [Houston, Soc. Stu., high g. 6, unit 1]

Do the pupils understand that there must be an enormous investment of capital and labor in any successful business enterprise? [Maryland, Soc. Stu., g. 4–6, p. 141]

REGULATION OF PUBLIC UTILITY COMPANIES

The Georgia Public Service Commission: its powers, its members. What does it control? What is its relation to transportation? [Georgia, General, g. 5, p. 212]

Who owns the railroads? the bus lines? Who regulates these public conveyances? [Minnesota, General, g. 4, p. 358]

By what ways does a city retain some control over its street car system? (p. 25) Why do cities usually give a franchise to only one street car company? To whom could you appeal if the street car company refused to run cars on your line except at rush hours when running cars is most profitable? (p. 27) [Houston, low g. 6, unit 1]

Generalization-to-be-developed: because we are so dependent upon light, heat, water, and power, they are partially controlled by the government. [Manhasset, *Tentative Social Studies Outline,* g. 5 and 6, p. 39. Not tabulated]

PROBLEMS ASSOCIATED WITH THE RISE OF BIG BUSINESS

Generalization-to-be-developed: the few tend to control the means of production. [Mississippi, p. 22, grade not specified]

Topic 44. Labor Organization. Its history and purposes; methods of advancing its ends; methods by which combatted.
General: primary 0%; intermediate 2%. Social Studies: primary 0%; intermediate 9%.

In most courses where this topic occurs it is found in a unit on medieval times, and involves comparison, not always accurate, between medieval guilds and modern labor unions.

What was the guild system? Do we have anything like the guild system today? Compare labor unions with the guilds. (Guilds looked after the interests of anyone who bought and sold goods. The object of the labor unions of today is to protect the interest of the workers alone through standardizing wages and limiting working hours. Unless demands of the union are met strikes and picketing are ordered.) [Delaware, Soc. Stu., g. 4, p. 151]

Are labor unions any help in solving the problem of unemployment? Are labor unions a new thing in history? Read about the trade guilds of the Middle Ages to see if they are in any way similar to our labor unions. In what ways are they different? [Houston, Soc. Stu., g. 5, unit 1, p. 7]

Comparing the present development of the union movement with its feudal beginnings in the guild. Calling in people from the community to help in the understanding of present and past labor organization. [Glencoe, General, g. 5, p. 52]

Teacher develops an understanding of the causes of the growth of labor unions and the chief things the unions work for: higher wages, shorter working hours, and better working conditions. Suggested reports: American Federation of Labor, Samuel Gompers, United States Department of Labor. [Berkeley, Soc. Stu., g. 5, p. 306]

Read to find out about: the coal miners' unions, wages, hours of work, work days, work hazards, labor problems in the mining industry, strikes, and lockouts. [Kansas, Soc. Stu., g. 6, pp. 295–9]

Topic 45. Distribution of Income; Concentration of Wealth.
General: primary 0%; intermediate 3%. Social Studies: primary 0%; intermediate 4%.

This topic is developed more fully in the South Dakota bulletin on social studies for intermediate grades than in any other bulletin, receiving incidental mention on three grade levels.

Compare the distribution of wealth in the Greek and Roman nations with the distribution of wealth in our own country. Why was there no great inequality at that time? Give arguments for and against a more equitable distribution of wealth. (g. 4, pp. 237–8) Did all classes of people benefit equally from the new discoveries made during medieval times? How did the use of the new kinds of goods affect the lives of the people in each class of European society? How does a new discovery or invention affect people in the different classes of society today? (g. 5, p. 515) Why are there bread lines when there is plenty of food? (g. 6, p. 711) Farmers, who pay heavy and disproportionate taxes on land, do not receive a proportionate part of the national income. (g. 6, p. 737) [South Dakota, Soc. Stu.]

In what ways can we provide for a more equitable distribution of wealth in our own age? (g. 4, unit 3, p. 7) How is our government trying to improve our methods of distribution so that all may have a fair share in the products of our physical environment? (low g. 6, unit 3, p. 2) [Houston, Soc. Stu.]

Understandings that may be developed: Our material prosperity has been attained under the capitalistic system; its methods for distributing goods, based upon the profit principle, tend to direct social products into the hands of the few. The minority of wealth derived from business and industry has succeeded the landed aristocracy. [Virginia, General, pp. 10–1, grade not specified.]

Topic 46. Our Prospects of Attaining an Adequate Standard of Living for All.

General: primary 0%; intermediate 4%. Social Studies: primary 0%; intermediate 0%.

Of all the courses examined, only four give any attention to this topic, and one of these (Virginia) suggests no methods for developing it. All the materials found are given below, together with a unit title from the Texas course of study which might bear upon this topic.

In order for the children to appreciate the growth and benefits of manufacturing, list the comparisons of the complex living of now with the simple living of George Washington's days. . . . Boys and girls should also see the offsetting effects of overspecialization. . . . They should understand: that mass production makes it possible to have things cheaply but it may exceed the limit of the people's ability to buy; that the failure of people to buy means laying off laborers; that in a land of plenty no one need be hungry or cold or roofless; that therein lies the desirability of controlled production. [Hamilton County *Yearbook, 1936–37*, g. 6, p. 131. Credit given to Virginia course of study for list of desired understandings.]

In a land of plenty no one need be hungry or cold or roofless. [Virginia, General, g. 6, p. 180]

Unit: "The United States as a Promising Environment." Aim: to survey the possibilities of the United States to supply man's needs, food, shelter, clothing, fuel, materials from which to make tools and equipment, favorable climate and luxuries. Problems: What do the people in your county need to make their lives happy and successful? How many kinds of workers are necessary to supply these needs? What kinds of natural resources are necessary to satisfy these needs? Make a comprehensive list in answer to each of these problems. On a map of the county locate towns, natural resources, and special features. How many people are there in the United States? Where do they live? What do they do? Who are they? Can the United States satisfy their needs? Draw a very large map of the United States; insert locations of natural resources, physical and regional areas, population areas, etc. [Missouri, General, g. 5, pp. 911–12]

What are our resources in materials and labor for providing good housing? [Missouri, General, g. 4, p. 910]

"Investigating the Problem of Our Country's Resources and Equipment in Fulfilling Our Need for Employment." [Texas, General, g. 6, p. 86]

Note: The above unit title might be developed so as to contribute to topic 46. No suggestions for teaching the unit are offered in the course of study.

COMMENTS ON GROUP V

Since Group I, Industries and Occupations in the Modern World, has the highest average frequency per topic, namely 159, it is strange that Group V, Characteristics of a Machine Civilization, should rank fifth, with an average frequency per topic of only 64. One would have expected that in the study of industries and occupations in the modern world such topics as "How machines have changed our ways of living," "Mass production and specialization," and "Labor conditions and problems" would often be mentioned, if not on the primary, certainly on the intermediate level.

One topic in Group V, Interdependence, ranks fourth among the entire list of fifty-six topics. The high rank of this topic in conjunction with the low rank of most topics in the group suggests that many course of study writers do indeed desire that our machine civilization be interpreted to children in the elementary school, but that they have not looked closely enough at its characteristics to see what basic understandings other than interdependence might be important.

Inasmuch as "Interdependence" is fourth in rank, and appears nearly as often on the primary level as on the intermediate, one is not prepared for the discovery that it occurs in only 55 per cent of the 420 general and social studies courses tabulated. So simple and so basic a topic might well have been expected in every course that is aimed at helping children understand the world in which they live. The absence of this topic from 45 per cent of the courses is related to the fact that in some of them the social studies program consists of separate and formal outlines in geography and history, in which the content is set forth to be memorized rather than used in interpreting present-day life.

"How machines have changed our ways of living" is another simple but important topic in which children show interest as early as the first grade. Yet it occurs in only 22 per cent of the courses tabulated.

"Mass production and specialization" occurs only one-third as often as the topic "How machines have changed our ways of living." But mass production and specialization are two of the principal ways in which machines have changed our ways of living. Surely the ideas are very simple; they are, as a matter of fact, presented on the primary level in five courses. There seems no good reason for the omission of this topic from two-thirds of those courses on the intermediate level which include the topic "How machines have changed our ways of living."

The low rank of the topic "Mass production and specialization" is still more striking when one compares its position of forty-sixth in the list of topics with that of "Manufacturing," which is fifth. It would be natural and illuminating to introduce the ideas of mass production and specialization or division of labor during the study of manufacturing. The failure to do so suggests that many course of study writers have no clear notion of the important understandings to which the study of manufacturing should contribute.

"Comparative standards of living" can be presented quite simply, as the materials on p. 121 show, and the topic is a very natural one to develop in the study of foreign countries and historical periods, both of which are universally studied in the intermediate grades. Moreover, it is not controversial. Its appearance in only 11 per cent of the courses tabulated raises the question whether enough attention is being given to the scientific as opposed to the picturesque phases of geography and history. The picturesque tends to dominate. For example, one gets the impression from some elementary social studies courses that the principal items to learn about The Netherlands are the use of wooden shoes and windmills, and that the principal characteristics of the Middle Ages were castle life and chivalry.

Inasmuch as "Industries and Occupations in the Modern World" is, numerically, the most important group of topics, and occupational orientation is an avowed objective in numerous courses of study, one is puzzled to find that the topic "Labor conditions and problems" occurs in only 10 per cent of the courses. If children are old enough to study an occupation, are they too young to discuss in simple terms such items as wages, hours of work, steadiness of employment, and healthfulness of the working conditions in that occupation? In two courses this topic is presented on the primary level, and judging from the sample materials given on pp. 122–3, there seems no reason why children in any intermediate grade should not consider the topic during their study of an industry or occupation.

Since the writers of 10 per cent of the courses include at least some phases of the topic "Labor conditions and problems," it is interesting that the topic "Unemployment" is mentioned in but 4 per cent and the topic "Labor organization" in less than 3 per cent of the courses. With respect to the topic "Unemployment," is there a feeling that if it is not discussed by their teachers, elementary children can be saved from worrying about it? With respect to the topic "Labor organization," is there a belief that if the school permits it to be discussed it is taking sides in the struggle between capital and labor, whereas if the topic is kept out of the classroom the school is demonstrating its neutrality?

The low rank of two of the topics in Group V, "Growth of big business; regulation of business" and "Distribution of income; concentration of wealth," may be due to difficulty in making these ideas sufficiently simple and concrete for children in the elementary school. But this explanation can hardly be advanced in the case of the topic "Prospects of attaining an adequate standard of living for all." The idea that the United States has enough mineral resources, land, machines, industrious people, skilled workers, scientists, and business men to produce enough for all is a very simple one. It may be easier to grasp by a mind that has not been too long exposed to the ancient but strong traditions of scarcity which hamper adult thinking. Moreover, the idea of potential abundance, if it is to remake public policies, not only must be accepted intellectually but must become a conviction of our people. This constitutes a strong argument for presenting it in every grade, beginning in the first. That it is presented in less than one per cent of the courses may be a fact of calamitous significance for the future of our country.

GROUP VI. MONEY MANAGEMENT

Each of the six items in the group "Money Management" appears on the average in 28 (7 per cent) of the 420 social studies and general courses tabulated. In this respect the group ranks sixth.

These topics are closely related to consumer education and may be expected to increase economic competence to the extent that pupils learn to be more thrifty in buying, more cautious in responding to advertisements, more intelligent as to proper uses of consumer credit, more aware of the desirability of keeping personal accounts and follow-

TABLE VI

MONEY MANAGEMENT

Topics Related to Economic Competence Found in General and Social Studies Courses

NUMBER AND PER CENT OF COURSES IN WHICH TOPIC APPEARS*

TOPIC	COMBINED COURSES (420)		GENERAL COURSES (210)								SOCIAL STUDIES COURSES (210)							
	No.	%	1	2	3	4	5	6	Total	%	1	2	3	4	5	6	Total	%
47. Budgets	35	8	1	0	1	5	9	10	26	12	0	1	1	1	4	2	9	4
48. Cash accounts	35	8	1	1	2	6	10	14	34	16	0	0	0	0	0	1	1	0
49. Giving to worthy causes ...	33	8	4	4	1	4	4	6	23	11	7	1	2	0	0	0	10	5
50. Thrift in buying	31	7	3	3	4	3	4	4	21	10	2	1	0	1	3	3	10	5
51. Advertising: caution in responding to	27	6	2	2	2	4	4	6	20	10	1	0	0	1	1	4	7	3
52. Consumer credit: how to use	7	2	0	0	0	0	0	1	1	0.5	0	0	1	1	1	3	6	3

* A course is the program for a single grade. For each grade 35 general courses and 35 social studies courses were tabulated.

ing a personal budget, and more desirous of sharing in the support of worthy causes.

Elementary school children handle money and are aware of its importance. Undoubtedly they need guidance in its use.

COUNTING THE TOPICS IN GROUP VI

Counting the topics of this group revealed no difficulties worth noting, except at the outset in the case of one item, "Thrift." Although the development of thrift appears as an objective of many courses, only a few of them contain suggestions on how this may be accomplished. The most common suggestions—teaching care in the use of school supplies, and collecting savings bank deposits from the children—seem to indicate a rather narrow conception of thrift education. It was decided to substitute "Thrift in buying" for "Thrift," and to combine with the topic "Banking" in Group VII any material on investing. No count was made of suggestions for the depositing of money, unless a study of banking was also indicated, in which case the material was counted as "Banking."

MATERIALS FROM COURSES OF STUDY ILLUSTRATING THE CONTENT OF TOPICS IN GROUP VI LIKELY TO CONTRIBUTE TO ECONOMIC COMPETENCE

Topic 47. Budgets; Cost of Living.
General: primary 2%; intermediate 23%. Social Studies: primary 2%; intermediate 7%.

Budgeting occurs principally in arithmetic outlines. Consideration of the cost of living should accompany any study of budgeting, but as a rule it does not. For samples of materials on the cost of living, it was necessary to use arithmetic courses exclusively.

PERSONAL BUDGETS

We got the idea of a personal budget from a boy who had an allowance and kept a notebook of his expenses. Each child made a chart of his expenses for two weeks. [Springfield, Arithmetic, g. 4, p. 10]

Plan a personal budget, including savings; keep the budget for a definite period of time and report. Have an adult who keeps a budget visit the class and discuss this problem. When children do not have allowances, the essential steps in budgeting can be introduced if each child keeps an account of everything he buys and its cost. [Texas, General, g. 5, pp. 60–1]

MAKING A FAMILY BUDGET

Work out a budget for a family of five for one month allowing an income of $1,800 a year. [Muskogee, Arithmetic, g. 6, p. 185]

Make a budget for a family of four whose income is $300 a month. [Houston, Soc. Stu., high g. 6, unit 1, p. 33]

For different incomes, what is the proper apportionment of income to the items of expense? [Missouri, Arithmetic, g. 5, p. 95]

COST OF LIVING FOR A CHILD AND FOR A FAMILY

Estimating clothing needs, making clothing budget. (g. 4, p. 12) Listed each article to be bought for our Easter costumes. (Each child was allowed to plan on spending twelve dollars.) Then we went to town and found the cost of each article, comparing this with our original estimates. (g. 5, p. 22) [Springfield, Arithmetic]

Finding cost of an outfit of clothing for a school child. [Amarillo Arithmetic, g. 4, p. 137]

We arranged a menu for one day for a family of a given size, calculated the total cost, and the cost for one person, compared this with cost of eating out; kept records of the amount of food used by an average family in one week, and found the cost per person per day. [Springfield, Arithmetic, g. 6, p. 27]

Compute: cost of wardrobes for a family, cost of cleaning and pressing for a month, cost of lights for a year, year's upkeep of a house, of a car, total cost of furniture for a room, for a house, average cost of illness for a family during one year, cost of celebrating holidays, cost of recreation for a month and for a year, total cost of a vacation, cost of income tax, cost of taxes on a home. Use these figures in working out a family budget. [Oregon, Arithmetic, g. 4–6, pp. 30–4]

MISCELLANEOUS

Work out a problem showing the cost of smoking for a year. [Nevada, General, Vol. II, g. 5, p. 218]

Topic 48. Keeping Cash Accounts.
General: primary 4%; intermediate 29%. Social Studies: primary 0%; intermediate 0.9%.

This topic occurs principally in arithmetic outlines, and suggestions for teaching it are infrequent.

Keeping a record of supplies bought for the school store, and supplies sold. (g. 1 and 2, p. 36) Keeping accounts on school parties. Keeping accounts in connection with supplies used in school. (g. 4, p. 48) Keeping record of the cost of trips taken by the group to various places; of room expenses during the year. (g. 6, pp. 60–1) [Glencoe, General]

Keep personal accounts, listing sources of income and amounts under each heading, and expenditures or purchases. Balance the accounts. [Texas, General, g. 5, pp. 60–1]

Topic 49. Giving to Worthy Causes and to Persons Other than One's Own Family, and Friends.
General: primary 9%; intermediate 13%. Social Studies: primary 10%; intermediate 0%.

This topic is most often represented by the suggestion that a Thanksgiving or Christmas basket be given to a needy family. Less personal but more constructive types of giving are sometimes suggested, such as contributing to the Red Cross or the Community Chest or preparing articles for a hospital or an orphanage.

Planning, filling, and carrying Thanksgiving, Christmas, and Easter baskets to people in the community. Making toys and books to give to children in community hospitals. [Virginia, General, g. 2, p. 72]

Making and filling tarlatan stockings for a hospital, day nursery, or orphans' home. (g. 1, p. 54) Filling boxes for disabled soldiers. Sending valentines to children in a hospital. (g. 2, pp. 135–6) [Kansas City, Soc. Stu.]

Send a Thanksgiving basket to some needy person. Send Christmas and birthday gifts to elderly persons, orphans, etc. Join a national agency of sharing, such as the Red Cross. [Texas, General, g. 4–6, p. 90]

Visit several community service agencies. Find out about their history and their work. Discuss how boys and girls can help these agencies. [Allentown, g. 5 and 6, *Community Services and the Community Chest.* Not tabulated.[5]]

How can our community show its Thanksgiving spirit? We can report all the sick people we know. We can find out who needs food and clothing. We can send things to the children's hospital. We can plan a Thanksgiving dinner in the cafeteria. [Hamilton County *Yearbook, 1937–38*, g. 2, p. 109]

[5] Because giving to the Community Chest was not suggested in any of the courses of study included in the tabulation, this item was taken from a publication not tabulated.

Dressing a doll to be given to some underprivileged child for Christmas. Making of toys to be given away to promote the spirit of giving without expecting something in return. [Hamilton County *Yearbook,* 1936–37, g. 6, p. 152]

Topic 50. Thrift in Buying.
General: primary 10%; intermediate 10%. Social Studies: primary 3%; intermediate 7%.

Recommendation for practice in wise buying through the expenditure of school funds is extremely rare. Talking about wise buying is suggested only a little more frequently.

ACTUAL BUYING UNDER SCHOOL GUIDANCE

Planning expenditure of money won as a P. T. A. prize or earned at a candy sale; comparing values. [Long Beach, Arithmetic, g. 4–6, p. 32]

Buying items needed for the school store. [Glencoe, General, g. 1–2, pp. 36–7]

Planning how to spend the library funds for books and magazines. [Illinois, Arithmetic, g. 4–6, p. 31]

Purchasing material for costumes and doll dresses. Purchasing supplies for a party. [Muncie, General, g. 3, p. 137]

TALKING ABOUT WISE BUYING

List some things that you have bought not because you needed or wanted them, but because of their being advertised or because you saw some one else with them. List some luxuries of modern homes that do not add to the health or comfort of the family. What is meant by wise spending? [Houston, Soc. Stu., g. 5, unit 3, p. 19]

The children kept an account of the money spent each day and week for lunches and candy. We compared the amounts spent for each. [Springfield, Arithmetic, g. 3, p. 5]

How can we distinguish between real and artificial needs, our wants and what others tell us we want, and our needs and our wants? [Missouri, General, g. 6, p. 939]

How can we buy coal to better advantage? (By buying early, by ordering in large quantities, by knowing the advantages of different kinds of coal.) [Springfield, Soc. Stu., g. 5, p. 140]

Discuss fake bargain sales and unwise economy that considers price alone without thought of probable service. [New Jersey, Arithmetic, g. 6, p. 169]

Topic 51. Caution in Responding to Advertising.
General: primary 6%; intermediate 13%. Social Studies: primary 1%; intermediate 6%.

This topic occurs in a small percentage of courses, and in most of these the treatment is very brief. Much the fullest treatment found is that of Arkansas, quoted in the fourth paragraph below.

Studying advertisements to learn how to tell a real bargain from an apparent bargain. (unit 3, p. 57) Discuss the question, "How do merchants try to create a demand for their products? (unit 1, p. 33) [Houston, Soc. Stu., high g. 6]

Find and bring to class advertisements of manufactured products. Discuss the accuracy of these as a true description of the products. [Binghamton, Soc. Stu., g. 6, *How Manufacturing Supplies Our Needs and Wants*, p. 23]

Collecting trademarks to illustrate a discussion of their use and significance. [Virginia, General, g. 6, p. 194]

Discussing the importance of advertising as it affects the consumers' choice of goods. Interviewing the manager of a store to find out how advertising affects trade. Discussing whether printed or radio advertising is more effective. Writing the American Medical Association for information on the quality and character of advertised drugs and medical appliances. Reading labels carefully and comparing them with the advertising matter. Collecting a large number of advertisements and verifying or disproving their claims by accounts of the use of the goods advertised. Testing some of the goods advertised. Discussing advertisements which make extravagant claims. [Arkansas, General, g. 4–6, p. 183]

Topic 52. How to Use Consumer Credit.
General: primary 0%; intermediate 1%. Social Studies: primary 1%; intermediate 5%.

This is a rare topic, ranking fifty-fifth in the entire list.

Discuss: At some grocery stores you can charge your groceries and pay for them at a later time. Someone has to pay for all the groceries that are charged. If you don't pay for the groceries you charge, the grocer will have to pay for them. [Des Moines, Soc. Stu., g. 1, p. 201]

Discuss the question: Does installment-plan buying tend to make one more extravagant? Report how the installment plan of buying a house may be an advantage to those who cannot pay cash. (unit 1, p. 34) Studying prices offered by firms selling on the installment plan; working examples to show the real price paid for goods bought on time; finding out what per cent could be saved by buying on a cash basis. (unit 3, p. 57) [Houston, Soc. Stu., high g. 6]

Discuss the advantages and disadvantages of buying and selling on credit. Discuss why some stores are willing to give credit, why some people are not given credit. (p. 236) Compare the cost of furniture bought for cash and on the installment plan. Why is a carrying charge made? (p. 344) [Fort Worth, Arithmetic, g. 6]

When is the installment plan of buying wise? unwise? [South Dakota, Soc. Stu., g. 6, p. 711].

Find out about credit unions. List reasons for borrowing money that are justifiable and others that are probably unwise, and explain why. Figure out the interest paid on purchase of various articles by installment. [Minnesota, *A Suggested Unit on Co-operation for Upper Grades,* Pt. I, p. 11. Not tabulated]

COMMENTS ON GROUP VI

The most significant fact about this group of topics is the low frequency of their occurrence, each item appearing, on the average, in less than 7 per cent of the courses tabulated.

Five of the topics occur in a much larger proportion of general courses than of social studies courses, since they tend to be dealt with chiefly in arithmetic outlines. The sixth topic, "How to use consumer credit," though one would expect its development to involve arithmetic, is six times as frequent in social studies courses as in the general courses tabulated.

All six of the topics are considerably more important on the intermediate level than on the primary, though most of them occur to some extent in every grade. It is rather surprising to find that budgeting is considered as early as the first grade.

Taking only the 105 general courses for intermediate grades, each topic in the group occurs on the average in 15 courses or 14.5 per cent. This is a low percentage in view of the undoubted importance of these topics for personal economic competence and the ease with which they can be treated in the arithmetic program. One is forced to ask the questions: Why has the movement for thrift and consumer education had so little effect on courses of study? and why has the movement for a more functional type of arithmetic had no more effect?

So far as the elementary schools are concerned, it is certain that the advertising profession has no reason to complain. The topic "Caution in responding to advertisements" is mentioned in but 6 per cent of the 420 social studies and general courses tabulated, and as a rule the mention occurs once only and occupies no more than a line or two.

Less even than the advertisers, need those who benefit by installment selling anticipate any change in public opinion or buying practices, so far as elementary education is concerned. Less than 2 per cent of the general and social studies courses tabulated so much as mention the need of information on the use of any form of consumer credit.

With regard to the content of the topics in the courses read, the following comments may be made:

1. The study of budgeting is seriously weakened by the failure to accompany it with a consideration of the cost of living for an average family in the community. To budget a hypothetical family income of $300 a month without budgeting an average income as well can only be mis-educative.

2. Few courses recommend that actual practice in planning how to spend money and in shopping should be provided. Without such practice it is a question whether making a budget on paper, or talking about thrift in buying can be very effective. Yet a few courses demonstrate that it is not impossible for the school to provide opportunity for children to participate in the spending of funds for library books, school supplies, and the like. (See p. 136)

3. The content, as well as the low frequency of the topic "Giving to worthy causes," indicates a gap in education for democracy. Wide popular support of social service agencies, such as the Red Cross and the Community Chest, would seem to be one of the criteria for democracy. If wide popular support is to be obtained, the appropriate attitudes and appreciations must be nourished from an early age. It is disturbing that no suggestion of giving to the Community Chest was found in 420 courses, that giving to the Red Cross or to any other social service agency is rarely suggested, and that the only type of giving (other than to the child's own family and friends) mentioned in most of the courses in which the topic occurs is of the Thanksgiving basket variety.

This situation reveals a gap not only in education for democracy but in character education as well. In an increasingly cooperative and interdependent society, people should find personal satisfaction in the voluntary support of agencies for social service. The alternative is the taking over by the government of an increasingly large proportion of the work of such agencies, and the further decline in the sense of individual responsibility for community welfare. The stress found in some courses on inducing children to save their pennies might better be applied to teaching the pleasure of giving to an organization serving children or families of the community.

GROUP VII. BUSINESS ORGANIZATION; BANKING

The four topics of this group were found on the average in 19 courses each, or 4.5 per cent of the total. If only intermediate grade courses are considered, the average frequency is 9 per cent. Numerically, this is the least important of the seven groups.

Knowledge of these four topics should increase a person's economic competence by:

1. Giving him an understanding of the services provided by banks.

2. Acquainting him with some of the simpler types of investments and the precautions to be taken before one makes an investment.

3. Acquainting him with the purposes of the cooperative movement and the methods by which a cooperative enterprise is organized and managed.

4. Acquainting him with the principal arguments for and against an extension of government ownership.

5. Giving him insight into the manner in which a private enterprise, especially a corporation, is financed, organized, and controlled.

It is not thought that the elementary school can do more in this area than create an awareness of and an interest in the work of banks, and the differences between private, cooperative, and government-owned enterprise.

COUNTING THE TOPICS IN GROUP VII

This group of topics proved rather difficult to define and to count.

Some mention of banks occurs in most courses. It was decided, however, to look for a consideration of the varied services of banks and not to count a reference dealing only with savings deposits. The topics

TABLE VII

BUSINESS ORGANIZATION; BANKING

Topics Related to Economic Competence Found in General and Social Studies Courses

TOPIC	COMBINED COURSES (420)		GENERAL COURSES (210)								SOCIAL STUDIES COURSES (210)							
			Grades								Grades							
	No.	%	1	2	3	4	5	6	Total	%	1	2	3	4	5	6	Total	%
53. Banks: varied services of ...	33	8	0	0	0	2	2	21	25	12	0	0	0	2	2	4	8	4
54. Cooperatives	17	4	0	0	0	0	1	2	3	1	0	0	2	1	2	9	14	7
55. Government ownership ...	15	4	0	0	0	2	3	4	9	4	0	0	1	1	2	3	6	3
56. Organization of private enterprise	11	3	0	0	0	0	0	3	4	2	1	0	0	1	2	3	7	3

* A course is the program for a single grade. For each grade 35 general courses and 35 social studies courses were tabulated.

NUMBER AND PER CENT OF COURSES IN WHICH TOPIC APPEARS *

"Borrowing money," "Investing," and "Checks of various kinds" were combined with "Banking" when it became clear that these occur infrequently.

Treatment of cooperatives and of government ownership is rare. It was decided to count any mention of cooperatives, regardless of its slightness, and to count any mention of the existence of government-owned business and its differences from businesses that are privately owned.

MATERIALS FROM COURSES OF STUDY ILLUSTRATING THE CONTENT OF TOPICS IN GROUP VII LIKELY TO CONTRIBUTE TO ECONOMIC COMPETENCE

Topic 53. Banks, Services of; Investing.
General: primary 0%; intermediate 25%. Social Studies: primary 0%; intermediate 8%.

The suggestion that children be urged to deposit money in a savings account was not counted as an occurrence of this topic, nor was the topic looked for below grade four. As defined above, the topic deals with the varied services of banks, not the mere receiving of deposits, and with investing. Consideration of investing, however, was indicated in very few courses.

Visiting the local bank to ask questions about its services and the way checks are handled, and to see the vault, safety deposit boxes, and other mechanical devices used. Arranging a display of bank books and other forms used in a bank. Organizing a school bank. Investigating and reporting on our postal savings system. Learning about the Federal Reserve Banks. [Mississippi, General, g. 6, pp. 280–8]

Find out the difference between a commercial bank and a savings bank. How does one open an account at a bank? draw money from a checking account? from a savings account? How does a bank make its money? How does the government control the banks? List ways in which the banks of Houston aid the city in carrying on its affairs. [Houston, Soc. Stu., high g. 6, unit 1, pp. 30–3]

Take up the building and loan association as a profitable investment and an aid to consistent saving. Consider share cost, premium, gross cost, interest, withdrawal privileges, etc. [New Jersey, Arithmetic, g. 6, p. 171]

A child brought up the subject of receiving interest on money at the bank. This led to discussion of interest on bonds, postal savings, and borrowed money. The reason for borrowing money for only thirty or sixty days was brought up. [Springfield, Arithmetic, g. 6, p. 30]

A committee studied means of exchange which may be used while traveling. Reports were given on drafts, traveler's, cashier's, certified, and personal checks. [Minneapolis, Arithmetic, g. 6, p. 89]

Topic 54. Cooperatives, Purposes of; Differences from Other Types of Enterprise.
General: primary 0%; intermediate 3%. Social Studies: primary 2%; intermediate 11%.

The topic typically occurs as a consideration of cooperative marketing in the study of the Scandinavian countries. In a few cases consideration of cooperative marketing in our country is indicated. No mention was found of consumer cooperation except in the Minnesota bulletin quoted.

Why are Iowa farmers interested in Denmark's cooperative farming? What is cooperative farming? [Iowa, Geography, g. 5 and 6, p. 136]

In what ways have cooperative societies helped to solve some of the difficulties of marketing dairy products, eggs, and bacon in Denmark and in the United States? Imagine you are a dairy farmer in Denmark. Contrast the difference in marketing your dairy products, eggs, and bacon since you have had cooperative societies with the time when there were none. [Ossining, g. 6, *The Animal Industries,* pp. 11–13. Not tabulated]

Of what value are fruit-growers' associations and cooperative societies? [Binghamton, g. 6, *How Agriculture Supplies Our Needs and Wants,* p. 17]

Writing stories of how pioneers in the local community cooperated in building houses, churches, roads, etc. Discussion of how Indians conducted informal tribal cooperatives. Organization of informal cooperative activities for the improvement of school grounds, for serving a school lunch, or other projects. (p. 6) Preparation of booklets showing history and present development of local cooperatives. Exchanging letters and booklets on local cooperatives with other schools in the state. Making a chart to show what kinds of goods people in your community can obtain through cooperatives. Drawing up a list of questions which one should ask to find out whether or not an organization is a real cooperative. (pp. 7–8) Making a diagram showing the similarities and differences between cooperatives and private corporations. Comparing cooperative activity with government activity. (pp. 9–10) Writing reports showing how rural life is being or may be improved by cooperative enterprise, such as telephone associations, electric lines, etc. [Minnesota, *A Suggested Unit on Cooperation for Upper Grades, Part I,* Not tabulated]

Topic 55. Government Ownership.

General: primary 0%; intermediate 9%. Social Studies: primary 0%; intermediate 6%.

Sometimes this topic indicates a discussion of the arguments for and against government ownership. Sometimes it merely points out that the government is engaged in business and shows some of the differences between a government-owned business and a private business.

Why do the people of Mexico want Mexico to keep the ownership of her own oil fields? [Sandusky, Soc. Stu., g. 6, no paging]

Why is our postal service not run for profit? Who owns the air-mail lines? Can you give reasons? [New Rochelle, Science, g. 6. Not tabulated]

Pupils may find out and report why private power companies oppose federal and city-owned power plants. [Mississippi, General, g. 6, pp. 267–8]

Resolved, that the city should own and manage its public utilities, including waterworks, electric light works, gas works, and street railways. [Washington, General, g. 4–6, p. 397]

Who owns the electric plants? If the government owned and operated them, should we have cheaper and better service, or does the competition of different companies give more satisfactory results? [South Dakota, Soc. Stu., g. 5, p. 443]

Should the irrigation projects in the West be government projects? (p. 15) Read news items concerning the controversy over the development of Muscle Shoals on a government owned and controlled basis. (p. 38) [Lakewood, Soc. Stu., g. 5]

Investigate the electric rates in the Tennessee Valley and in communities where there is municipal ownership. Discuss and compare these rates with ours. [Fort Worth, Arithmetic, g. 6, p. 247]

Topic 56. How a Private Enterprise Is Organized and Managed.

General: primary 0%; intermediate 4%. Social Studies: primary 1%; intermediate 6%.

Most occurrences of this topic are in fifth and sixth grade courses, but one is in a fourth grade and one, surprisingly, in a first grade course.

Who owns the grocery stores in Des Moines? (Some are owned by one person, some by two persons called partners, and some by several people called a company. Some are called chain stores because there are others like them owned by the same company.) [Des Moines, Soc. Stu., g. 1, p. 201]

Make up a story of boys and girls going into partnership and sharing the money earned. [Muncie, Arithmetic, g. 5, p. 98]

How business is managed. Businesses run by a single individual; partnerships; corporations; how a corporation is formed and carried on; trusts; comparison of a corporation and a cooperative. [Missouri, General, g. 6, p. 945]

Read to learn how corporations develop and the purpose they serve in modern exchange. [Houston, Soc. Stu., high g. 6, unit 1, p. 30]

Develop the story of the growth of corporations. Discuss differences between a partnership and a corporation. Find out from local storekeepers and milk distributors whether their businesses are conducted by corporations, partnerships, or individual ownership. [Berkeley, Soc. Stu., g. 5, p. 306]

A school bank was set up by pupils, organized, and operated. Papers of incorporation and a charter were drawn, stock was sold, a board of directors was elected by the stockholders, and bank officers were appointed by the directors. [Idaho, Arithmetic, p. 5. Grade not specified]

COMMENTS ON GROUP VII

That the four topics on business practices and organizations fall in the lowest quarter of the fifty-six topics and two of them fall in the lowest tenth, is the most striking thing about this group. It should be noted, however, that three of the topics occur only in intermediate courses, and all four occur more often in the sixth than in any lower grade. Evidently they are regarded as difficult.

That these topics can be made sufficiently simple and concrete to be meaningful to fifth and sixth graders is suggested by some of the sample materials on pp. 142–5. The materials on these pages are probably no more abstract than conventional materials in fifth or sixth grade courses in geography. As to the importance of these four topics compared with many of those that are conventional in courses for the intermediate grades, there would seem to be little room for argument.

In the study of the local community the attention of children might easily be directed to the manner in which some of the local businesses were started. Differences between a private business and one that is run by the government, as illustrated by the post office and the waterworks, might also be pointed out. If there are any businesses in or near the community that are run by cooperatives, the children might find out

TABLE VIII

ADDITIONAL TOPICS HAVING A BEARING UPON ECONOMIC COMPETENCE
FOUND IN GENERAL AND SOCIAL STUDIES COURSES*

HOUSEHOLD ECONOMY
  The principles of cookery
  The principles of food preservation
  Selection of meats; government grades; the various cuts
  Seasonal fluctuations of food prices

COMMUNITY SERVICES
  The non-governmental welfare agencies of the community
  The public welfare agencies of the community
  Relationship between an adequate supply of the necessaries of life and
    one's value to the community (Also cited on p. 98)
  Provisions for social security

ECONOMIC ASPECTS OF CRIME
  Cost of crime compared with school costs
  Relation of unemployment to crime

PRICES; WEALTH; INSURANCE
  Factors determining the price of a manufactured article
  Proportion of price consumer pays that goes for distribution cost
  Meaning of the term "wealth"
  Sharing risks by means of insurance

LAND TENURE; ECONOMIC PLANNING
  Methods of acquiring and owning land
  Reasons for zoning rural land
  Arguments for economic planning

ECONOMIC ASPECTS OF FOREIGN AFFAIRS
  Cost of a battleship
  Cost of the World War
  Economic facts in American foreign relations
  Economic reasons for the maintenance of the British Empire

---

* None of these topics were found in social studies courses and general courses from more than two places.

how they differ from businesses run by private enterprise. Without question children can be taught to observe and take an interest in the various types of business organization by the time they reach fourth or fifth grade. It would appear, therefore, that course of study writers for the intermediate grades have neglected, in units on industries and occupations, an opportunity to build appreciations and understandings of the American economic structure.

ADDITIONAL TOPICS FOUND IN GENERAL AND SOCIAL STUDIES COURSES

During the analyses of general and social studies courses a number of topics were found which could not be readily combined with any of the topics on the check list. These additional topics were noted on small cards. None of them occurred in courses from more than two places. They are given in Table VIII, which also includes equally rare topics from the original list of eighty.

Topics found in the arithmetic and science outlines contained in general courses were not included in this table. Their range is indicated by Tables IX to XII, in which are listed topics from separately published arithmetic and science courses.

COMMENTS ON TABLE VIII

Some of the items in Table VIII could be readily incorporated in such commonly taught units as "Foods," "Farming," and "The Local Community." Others are typical of learnings which the teacher trained in economics may introduce incidentally during the discussion of current events.

COMMENTS ON TOPICS AND MATERIALS AS A WHOLE

For detailed comments regarding each group of topics, see pp. 78–80, 96–8, 104–5, 112–3, 129–31, 138–40, and 145–6. The following comments apply to the topics and materials as a whole.

1. Materials likely to contribute to economic competence were found in some courses which did not have objectives bearing on economic competence.

2. Some of the sample materials are couched in adult language. Only the well-qualified teacher will know how to clothe such abstractions with meaning for children.

3. In some instances, few samples could be found which suggested experiences for developing the topics. If these topics are to be successfully taught, teachers must devise ways for relating them to the experiences and observations of children.

CHAPTER FIVE

Topics Bearing on Economic Competence Found in Arithmetic and Science Courses

IN order to obtain further information on the economic content of elementary courses of study it was decided to analyze samples of arithmetic and science courses. Although the list of fifty-six topics had strained out but a portion of the economic content of the arithmetic and science outlines included in the general courses tabulated, it seemed best for the present purpose to use only arithmetic and science courses issued as separate bulletins.

METHODS OF ANALYSIS

The method used in analyzing the arithmetic and science courses differed somewhat from that used with the general and social studies courses. A tentative list of topics was not made out in advance. Instead, during the reading of the courses each topic that appeared to have bearing on economic competence was, when encountered for the first time, noted on the tabulation sheet. On its first appearance in any other course of study a check was placed alongside the entry. When completed the record showed the number of courses in which each topic had been found at least once. Two lists were made, one for arithmetic and one for science courses. Afterward, the topics appearing in courses from fewer than three places were placed on separate lists. (See Tables X and XII.)

I. TOPICS IN ARITHMETIC COURSES

THE ARITHMETIC SAMPLE

Courses for grades four, five, and six only were used in the sample since inspection revealed that the economic content of arithmetic courses for use below the fourth grade is negligible. It had been intended to use no bulletins published before 1930, but in order to improve the geographic representativeness of the sample, three earlier bulletins were added. These were: State of New York, 1924; Vermont, 1928; and Baltimore, 1929, with a supplement issued in 1931.

One hundred fourteen arithmetic courses were analyzed, thirty-eight each for grades four, five, and six. These represent thirteen states, one county, and twenty-four cities of various sizes, with an aggregate population in 1930 of approximately forty-nine million. The places are well distributed throughout the northeastern area and the area west of the Mississippi, but the Southeast is represented only by the cities of Greensboro, North Carolina, and Charleston, South Carolina.

The data obtained in the analysis of the arithmetic courses are presented in Tables IX and X.

In Table IX the groups are arranged in descending order of importance according to the average frequency of topics in each group. The topics within a group are also arranged in descending order of importance according to their frequency.

TABLE IX

TOPICS BEARING ON ECONOMIC COMPETENCE AND THE NUMBER AND PER CENT OF 114 ARITHMETIC COURSES IN WHICH THEY APPEAR

TOPICS	Grades			Total	Per Cent
	4	5	6		
I. COST OF VARIOUS ITEMS OF LIVING*					
1. Vacations and excursions	8	12	7	27	24
2. Lunches, picnics, meals out	9	8	7	24	21
3. Automobile upkeep and travel	7	11	5	23	20
4. Recreations and recreation equipment	7	6	6	19	17
5. Clothing	6	8	5	19	17
6. Gardening: cost of and savings from	6	7	5	18	16
7. Food for family	6	6	5	17	15
8. Fuel for a family	5	3	6	14	12
9. Furnishings, appliances for a home	2	5	7	14	12
10. Shelter	3	5	5	13	11
11. Light for a family	3	3	6	12	11
12. Travel: comparative costs	2	3	5	10	9
13. Textiles: comparative costs	2	3	2	7	6
14. Pets: cost of keeping	1	2	4	7	6
15. Homemade vs. ready-made garments	0	1	2	3	3

* Only problems involving investigation of actual costs were counted.

TABLE IX (*Continued*)

TOPICS BEARING ON ECONOMIC COMPETENCE AND THE NUMBER AND PER CENT
OF 114 ARITHMETIC COURSES IN WHICH THEY APPEAR

TOPICS	GRADES			Total	Per Cent
	4	5	6		
II. MONEY MANAGEMENT;					
CONSUMER-BUSINESS PRACTICES					
16. Accounts, personal	7	13	19	39	34
17. Bills and receipts	4	7	20	31	27
18. Budgets, personal	4	8	14	26	23
19. Sending money by mail	8	7	9	24	21
20. Budgets, family	5	5	11	21	18
21. Buying by mail	5	4	9	18	16
22. Savings made through sales and discounts	0	2	14	16	14
23. Computing postage for a package	3	5	6	14	12
24. Budgets, time	2	2	6	10	9
25. Shopping for low prices	2	4	2	8	7
26. Reading meters	0	1	6	7	6
27. Buying on installments	0	1	5	6	5
28. Discounting bills	0	0	5	5	4
29. Comparative costs of shipping	1	1	3	5	4
30. Comparative costs of communication	1	0	2	3	3
31. Borrowing money (personal loans)	0	0	3	3	3
III. BANKING					
32. Savings bank deposits; payment of interest	1	6	21	28	25
33. Checking accounts	1	3	7	11	10
34. Postal savings system	0	2	4	6	5
35. Building-and-loan associations	0	0	4	4	4
IV. SCHOOL AND EDUCATION COSTS					
36. School supplies: cost of	10	4	5	19	17
37. School equipment and furnishings: cost of	3	2	3	8	7
38. An education or a course: cost of	2	2	4	8	7
39. School and library books: cost of	1	1	3	5	4
V. BUSINESS PRACTICES					
40. Accounts: enterprise	2	3	5	10	9
41. Selling and marketing farm products	2	1	6	9	8
42. Overhead costs in a store	2	1	1	4	4
43. Borrowing money for a business	0	0	3	3	3
VI. MISCELLANEOUS ECONOMIC INFORMATION					
44. Wages in a variety of occupations	3	3	4	10	9
45. Cost and economic value of government services	3	3	3	9	8
46. Taxation: kinds, how levied	1	1	3	5	4
47. Weights and measures: history of	0	0	3	3	3

TABLE X

ADDITIONAL TOPICS BEARING ON ECONOMIC COMPETENCE
FOUND IN 114 ARITHMETIC COURSES*

COST OF VARIOUS ITEMS OF LIVING
Shelter: comparative costs of owning vs. renting
Cooking: comparative costs of home-baked and purchased baked goods
Illness: cost of (medical care, nursing, hospital charges, loss of time)

MONEY MANAGEMENT; CONSUMER-BUSINESS PRACTICES
False bargains: avoiding of
Cash-and-carry stores: saving through buying at
Buying in quantity: resultant savings
Buying and selling a house
Telegrams: cost of
Sending money by telegraph or cable
Budget for a club

SCHOOL AND EDUCATION COSTS
Stenography, accounting, or secretarial work: cost and value of a
course in
Vocational or professional training: value of compared with other
investments

BUSINESS PRACTICES
Partnership as a form of business organization
Retailing and wholesaling: differences between
Inventory: making an
Advertising: cost of various kinds

MISCELLANEOUS ECONOMIC INFORMATION
Budget for a community
Freight rates to various points
Forest fires: cost of
Farms: cost of buying and equipping
Food production: costs of
Changes in the prices of food, clothing, and shelter since pioneer days
How the people of the United States spend each dollar
Money: history of
Money: requirements for sound paper money
Calendar reform: proposals for a new calendar

---

* None of these topics were found in arithmetic courses from more than two places.

COMMENTS ON TABLES IX AND X

The relation of each group of topics to economic competence and the ranking of each group is discussed below.

I. The Cost of Various Items of Living. To be economically competent an individual needs a clear idea of living costs for an average family. Children in the intermediate grades can begin to learn some of the facts about the cost of living. Thus they will come to appreciate the amount of money which their parents have to spend.

Exercises based on fictitious costs cannot be expected to contribute to an understanding of the cost of living; therefore, only exercises involving the investigation of actual costs were counted. Eighteen topics having to do with living costs were found, fifteen of which occur in courses from more than two places. These fifteen appear on the average in fifteen courses each or 13 per cent of the total. The most frequent, "Vacations and excursions," occurs in twenty-seven courses or 24 per cent of those analyzed. The cost of automobile upkeep and travel is taken up in 20 per cent of the courses, the cost of a home garden and the savings resulting therefrom in 16 per cent, the cost of keeping a pet in 6 per cent, and the cost of homemade as compared with ready-made garments in 3 per cent.

II. Money Management; Consumer-Business Practices. Knowledge of how to keep personal accounts, to make out and receipt a bill, to make a budget, to send money by mail, to take advantage of sales and discounts, to compute postage for a package, to read a meter, to select the most suitable means of shipping or communicating, and the like, should contribute appreciably to one's economic competence as a consumer.

Twenty-three items are included in this group, sixteen of which occur in courses from more than two places. Of these sixteen, each appears on the average in 14.6 courses or 13 per cent of the total. The most frequent topic of the entire list is "Personal accounts," which appears in 34 per cent of the courses. "Bills and receipts" is second on the entire list, appearing in 27 per cent of the courses.

III. Banking. Economic competence requires some acquaintance with the service of banks, and this should be supplemented with information about other institutions for saving, such as the postal savings system, building-and-loan associations, and credit unions.

Of the four items in this group each appears on the average in twelve courses, or 11 per cent of the total. Over half of the sixth grade courses in arithmetic give information about savings banks as a basis for problems in computing interest. Checking accounts are taken up in 10 per cent of the courses, while the postal savings system and building-and-loan associations are each mentioned half as often. It is deplorable that no mention of credit unions was found in the one hundred fourteen arithmetic courses examined.

IV. School and Education Costs. With some knowledge of school costs one may be expected to share more intelligently in decisions regarding the support of education. Information as to the cost of vocational or professional training may improve one's competence to plan his own education. There seems no reason why children in the intermediate grades might not be given information of this kind in connection with exercises in problem-solving.

Only six topics bearing on school and education costs were found, and only four of these appear in courses from more than two places. These four occur in ten courses each, on the average, or 9 per cent of the total. The most frequent topic in the group, "Cost of school supplies," appears in 17 per cent of the courses; the next most frequent, "Cost of school equipment and furnishing" and "Cost of an education or a course," each appear in 7 per cent of the courses.

The low rank of the topics in this group suggests that an opportunity is being missed to present important economic information that is within the experience of children.

V. Business Practices. Knowledge of business practices should make one a more efficient consumer of business services and give insight into the problems involved in running a business. In an economy based upon private enterprise, an understanding of business practices and the problems of the business man would seem to be very desirable.

Most arithmetic courses for intermediate grades are characterized by a complete lack of information on business. Only eight topics were found, and four of these occur in courses from no more than two places. The remaining four appear, on the average, in seven courses each, or 6 per cent of the total.

VI. Miscellaneous Economic Information. Fourteen topics fall into this category, but only four are mentioned in courses from more than two places, these four appearing in seven courses each on the average. The most frequent topic, "Wages in a variety of occupations," appears in ten courses, or 9 per cent of the total. That the number of topics in this group is no larger is more surprising than the low average frequency.

Summary of Comments on Tables IX and X. In studying these tables two facts stand out: (1) arithmetic courses include a wide variety of topics which may contribute to economic competence; (2) the number of courses in which each topic appears is small, in no case exceeding 34 per cent of the courses analyzed and the median for the topics in Table IX being only 8 per cent. It is evident, therefore, that the informational as distinguished from the computational content of arithmetic is not very important in most arithmetic courses for the intermediate grades.

II. TOPICS IN SCIENCE COURSES

THE SCIENCE SAMPLES

One hundred thirty-eight science courses were analyzed, twenty-three each for grades one through six. All were published since January 1, 1930, except the New York City bulletin dated 1927, and the Salt Lake City bulletin dated 1929. The sample includes bulletins issued by eleven states, two counties, and sixteen cities, with a population in 1930 of about forty-three million. The places are well distributed over every section of the country save the Southeast, which is represented only by South Carolina.

Because a considerable proportion of the science courses do not designate the content for each grade but only for "primary" grades or for "intermediate" grades, it was thought best to tabulate topics so designated in separate columns. Hence the first two columns of Table XI are marked "Primary" and "Intermediate," and in figuring the total, the items in these columns were multiplied by three before adding to the items in the six adjoining columns.

In Table XI the groups of topics are arranged in descending order of importance according to the average frequency of the topics in each.

TABLE XI

TOPICS BEARING ON ECONOMIC COMPETENCE AND NUMBER AND PER CENT OF 138 SCIENCE COURSES IN WHICH THEY APPEAR

TOPICS	PRIMARY[1]	INTERMEDIATE[2]	GRADES 1	2	3	4	5	6	TOTAL[3]	PER CENT
I. CONSERVATION										
1. Birds: attracting and protecting	6	5	8	13	8	9	11	6	88	64
2. value of	5	3	2	6	8	14	10	4	68	49
3. ways reduced	0	4	0	1	2	3	1	0	19	14
4. Wild flowers, protection of	6	4	5	6	9	6	7	4	67	49
5. Toads and frogs, value of	4	1	2	2	5	6	6	4	40	29
6. Forests: methods of conserving	2	3	0	0	3	4	9	7	38	28
7. value of	3	3	0	0	2	3	7	5	37	27
8. state and national	1	3	0	0	1	1	5	1	20	14
9. Soil: kinds, qualities	3	3	1	3	1	4	9	4	40	29
10. saving and building up	1	3	0	1	2	3	5	5	27	20
11. ways exhausted and wasted	1	2	0	0	3	3	3	4	22	16
12. Laws to protect wild life	3	2	0	2	4	6	5	4	36	26
13. Sanctuaries, wild life	4	3	0	0	3	4	3	2	33	24
14. Furbearers and game animals: ways reduced	2	2	0	2	2	5	4	2	27	20
15. protecting and increasing	1	3	1	1	2	3	4	2	24	17
16. Snakes, value of	2	1	1	1	3	6	2	4	26	19
17. Fish: ways reduced	3	2	1	0	1	0	2	1	20	14
18. protecting and increasing	1	4	0	0	4	2	6	3	28	20
19. Natural beauty, preservation of	2	2	0	0	0	3	3	0	18	13
20. Coal: ways wasted	2	2	0	0	0	0	1	1	8	6
21. conservation of	0	2	0	0	0	0	1	0	7	5
22. Petroleum: ways wasted	0	1	0	0	0	0	1	1	5	4
23. conservation of	0	1	0	0	0	0	2	0	5	4

II. AGRICULTURE AND HORTICULTURE

24. Gardening, vegetable	3	5	4	5	3	5	6	4	51	37
25. Gardening, flower	2	3	3	2	3	5	2	6	36	26
26. Weed control	2	2	1	1	4	2	3	3	26	19
27. Ornamental trees, shrubs, vines	2	1	0	1	0	2	2	3	17	12
28. Horticultural pests, control of	1	0	1	1	1	1	5	4	16	12
29. Irrigation: methods, value	0	1	0	0	1	1	4	2	11	8
30. Fruit growing	1	1	0	0	1	0	0	1	8	6
31. Poultry, care of	0	1	0	0	0	0	1	1	5	4

III. WATER SUPPLY

32. Sources of drinking water	2	4	0	1	3	2	2	7	33	24
33. Purification of water	0	3	0	0	2	2	3	3	19	14
34. Hard and soft water	0	1	0	0	0	1	1	2	7	5

IV. ELECTRICITY

35. Where and how produced	0	2	0	2	1	2	2	3	16	12
36. Importance and value	2	2	0	2	1	0	1	1	17	12
37. Fuses: purposes, use	0	1	0	1	0	1	1	1	7	5

V. HOUSEHOLD SCIENCE

38. Food selection	3	3	2	4	1	3	3	1	32	23
39. Ventilating a home	1	1	3	2	3	1	2	0	17	12
40. Heating a home; fuels	1	1	2	1	1	3	4	2	19	14
41. Clothes, selection to suit weather	2	0	3	4	2	1	1	0	17	12

TABLE XI (*Continued*)

Topics Bearing on Economic Competence and Number and Per Cent of 138 Science Courses in Which They Appear

TOPICS	PRIMARY[1]	INTERMEDIATE[2]	GRADES						TOTAL[3]	PER CENT
			1	2	3	4	5	6		
42. Food preservation, principles of	1	0	1	0	0	0	1	5	10	7
43. Pests, household, control of	0	1	0	0	0	1	1	2	7	5
44. Lighting a home	0	1	0	0	2	1	0	1	7	5
45. Soaps and cleansers	1	0	0	0	0	1	1	1	6	4
46. Textiles, recognizing the kinds	1	0	0	1	0	0	2	0	6	4
47. Textiles, detailed properties	0	0	0	1	1	0	2	0	4	3
VI. MISCELLANEOUS										
48. Fire: prevention, control	1	2	4	3	2	2	4	1	25	18
49. Fly control	2	1	0	0	1	4	3	1	18	13
50. Mosquito control	2	0	0	2	1	4	4	1	18	13
51. Poisonous plants: recognition, control	1	2	0	1	3	2	0	2	17	12
52. Lumber: kinds, uses	0	1	0	0	0	3	2	1	9	7
53. Other building materials	0	0	0	0	2	0	1	1	4	3

1 Content for grades one through three where exact grade level is not indicated.

2 Content for grades four through six where exact grade level is not indicated.

3 The items in the first two columns, marked "Primary" and "Intermediate," have been multiplied by three before adding to the items in the six adjoining columns.

158

TABLE XII

ADDITIONAL TOPICS HAVING A BEARING ON ECONOMIC COMPETENCE
FOUND IN SCIENCE COURSES*

CONSERVATION
Conservation of Christmas greens

HOUSEHOLD SCIENCE
Principles of cookery
What milk grades mean
How the community guards the food supply
Sewage disposal

ELECTRICITY
How to read an electric meter
Cost of running electric appliances

MISCELLANEOUS
How to use a camera
How to control rodents
How use of by-products increases the nation's wealth
How use of machine power has raised the standard of living
How quantity production provides us with many luxuries
Various sources of power and where each is used

* None of these topics were found in science courses from more than two places.

Within the first group, Conservation, some of the topics fall into sub-groups pertaining to birds, forests, soil, fur bearers and game animals, fish, coal, and petroleum respectively. These sub-groups are arranged in descending order of importance according to the average frequency of the topics in each. In the remaining groups the topics are arranged in descending order of importance according to their individual frequency.

COMMENTS ON TABLES XI AND XII

The relation of each group of topics to economic competence and the relative frequency of the topics in science courses is discussed below.

I. Conservation. Information that increases understanding of the importance of conservation and the methods by which individuals and communities may promote it, should add to one's economic competence as a citizen. It is to this aspect of economic competence that science courses make their principal contribution. Twenty-four conservation topics were found, twenty-three of which appear in courses from more than two places. These twenty-three appear on the average in thirty-one courses each or 22 per cent of the total.

"Protection of birds" and "Protection of wild flowers" are by far the most frequent of the conservation topics, undoubtedly because they are the closest to the hearts of children. It is interesting to find conservation of soil ranking above that of fur bearers and game animals, snakes, and fish, for this suggests that importance to society rather than the spontaneous interest of children in wild life has been the criterion of selection.

The low rank of the topic "Preservation of natural beauty" (found in 13 per cent of the courses) is probably due not to lack of social importance or interest to children but to the fact that aesthetic values are not considered the concern of science. However, this phase of conservation has considerable economic significance and deserves serious attention either in science or in social studies or in both. It is getting little attention in either area.

The very low rank of the topics related to the conservation of coal and petroleum, and the absence of any mention of the need to conserve metals, should be noted. Since mining is taken up in 38 per cent of the general and social studies courses analyzed, there seems no good reason why the conservation of minerals should be so rarely mentioned in both social studies and science courses.

II. Agriculture and Horticulture. A considerable proportion of science courses, as in the case of general courses and social studies courses, contain materials designed to improve methods of farming or to encourage the home production of the family's food supply. These materials should tend to increase the economic competence of rural dwellers.

Eight topics were found that deal with various phases of agriculture or horticulture, and these appear on the average in 16 per cent of the courses. Vegetable gardening is the most frequent, occurring in 37 per cent of the science courses. Animal husbandry is considered in only one topic, "Care of poultry," found in 4 per cent of the courses.

III. Water Supply. Knowledge of how to obtain a supply of safe drinking water is of considerable economic importance to rural dwellers. Information on the differences between hard and soft water may be of economic value, especially in laundering. Each of the three topics having to do with the water supply occurs on the average in 14 per cent of the science courses analyzed, making this the third most important group.

IV. Electricity. Information on the cost of running electric appliances, the reading of a meter, and the changing of fuses may be expected to improve the economic competence of users of electricity. Information on the value of electricity and how it is produced may improve one's economic competence as a citizen, since an important issue of the time is how the benefits of cheap current may be brought to all the people.

Of the five topics on electricity found in science courses, three occur in courses from more than two places, and each of these three appears on the average in but 9 per cent of the courses.

V. Household Science. This group of topics should promote economic competence with respect to the selection and use of goods, particularly clothing, fuels, insecticides, cleansing agents, and textiles. Of the twelve topics in the group, ten occur in courses from more than two places, and each of these ten appears on the average in 9 per cent of the courses.

VI. Miscellaneous Information of Economic Value. Twelve topics that appear likely to contribute to economic competence but do not fall in the preceding groups were found in science courses. Of the six that occur in courses from more than two places, the average frequency is 11 per cent. These deal with fire prevention, the control of flies, mosquitoes, and poisonous plants, and with lumber and other building materials. The six topics found in courses from fewer than three places suggest some other interesting contributions to economic competence. Instruction in "How to use a camera" should save money and increase the satisfaction of camera owners. "How to control rodents" is an economic problem in many households and on farms, and one with which children are familiar. The topics "How use of machine power has raised the standard of living" and "How quantity production provides us with many luxuries" are suggestive of some of those found in general and social studies courses under the heading "Characteristics of a machine civilization." The topic "Various sources of power and where each is used" may be of interest to fifth and sixth graders studying manufacturing, transportation, and other industries. It has an obvious bearing on the capacity of our economy to produce an adequate scale of living for all.

Summary of Comments on Tables XI and XII. Sixty-six topics from science courses are listed in Tables XI and XII, but the average frequency is low. Of the fifty-three topics in Table XI, the median item was found in only eighteen courses or 13 per cent of the total. The group of conservation topics is of far greater numerical importance than any other. The low rank of the "Household science" group is noteworthy; it suggests that most science courses for the first six grades are not concerned with everyday experiences in the home.

CHAPTER SIX

Conclusions and Recommendations

THE importance of educating the oncoming generation to understand the economic structure of the machine age and to participate effectively as producers, consumers, and citizens in its operation and control has impressed itself upon many thoughtful minds. The belief that education for this purpose must begin in the earliest years of schooling and continue well into adulthood has been expressed by various scholarly writers.

In the days of domestic and small-scale production, education for economic competence was not the task of the school. Children daily witnessed the economic activities of their elders, heard these activities planned and discussed, and began to share them at an early age. They saw the whole economic process from the production of the raw material to its manufacture, exchange, and ultimate consumption. They mastered the patterns of economic life in childhood.

Today, the economic patterns are much more varied and complex. It is difficult to see the relationships of the separate and specialized activities. Many economic activities are no longer carried on in the home or under the eyes of children. The economic structure is a mystery, not only to the child but to many adults. To dispel this mystery constitutes perhaps the greatest challenge that faces the schools in a democracy.

How much the elementary school does contribute to education for economic competence is not known, but there is reason to believe that its potential contribution is large. It shapes the child's basic attitudes and appreciations in his most impressionable years. If it perpetuates economic traditions that originated in an earlier and different economy —and this is bound to be the case where no thought has been given to the understandings which are needed to operate and control the economy of today—it may hamper the child seriously in his efforts to understand and participate, as producer, consumer, and citizen, in economic activity.

To explore the nature of the economic education now being given in the elementary school was the purpose of this study. The intention was to chart an uncharted field through analysis of a nation-wide sample of recent courses of study.

SUMMARY

Approximately nine hundred courses were read, or about one hundred fifty for each grade from one through six. With a few exceptions these were published between 1930 and 1939. A total of six hundred seventy-two courses were analyzed in detail; these represented four samples, general, social studies, arithmetic, and science courses respectively. The analysis has demonstrated that:

1. Many topics commonly treated in the elementary school may be the vehicles for learnings having a significant relation to economic competence.

2. A minority of course of study writers are already aware of the implications of these topics for economic competence.

3. Some existing courses of study contain a great deal of economic material that on the whole appears well adapted to the interests and abilities of elementary school children.

The four questions which the analysis of courses was designed to answer have been answered, and the findings are briefly reviewed below.

1. What general objectives bearing on economic competence are stated in courses of study for the first six grades? Fifteen principal objectives were found. (See pp. 34-5) The typical curriculum bulletin expresses only a few of these, the most common being: the practice of thrift, the conservation of material resources and property, a knowledge of common business terms and practices, occupational orientation, ability to select and use consumer goods, and understanding of social-economic problems.

2. In elementary courses what are the commonly occurring topics and activities most likely to be the vehicles for learnings having a

significant relation to economic competence? After listing the abilities and understandings thought necessary for economic competence (see pp. 8–10), search was made for topics and activities which might contribute to these learnings.

In general and social studies courses, out of a tentative initial list of eighty topics and activities, fifty-six were found in courses from two or more places. The median topic was found in eighty-two courses, or 19.5 per cent of the total, the range being from 75 to 0.9 per cent. In addition twenty-one topics were found in courses from one or two places.

In arithmetic courses forty-seven topics likely to contribute to economic competence were found in courses from more than two places, the median item appearing in 8 per cent of the courses, the range being from 34 to 3 per cent. In addition twenty-six topics were found in courses from one or two places.

In science courses fifty-three topics likely to contribute to economic competence were found in courses from more than two places, the median item occurring in 13 per cent of the courses, the range being from 57 to 3 per cent. Thirteen additional topics were found in courses from fewer than three places.

3. In how many courses and on what grade levels does each topic or activity appear at least once? The answer to this question is given in Tables I to VII, IX, and XI.

Considered alone, the tables might produce an exaggerated impression of the attention given to education for economic competence in the courses analyzed. It should be remembered that few or none of the implications of a given topic for economic competence may be brought out in some of the courses in which the topic appears, and all the implications of a given topic are brought out in but one or two of the courses in which it appears.

4. What course of study materials related to the topics selected from general and social studies courses are likely to contribute to economic competence? Problems and activities which are suggested in courses of study for the teaching of the fifty-six topics are presented in Chapter Four.

STRENGTHS AND WEAKNESSES OF THE
SITUATION FOUND

The strengths and weaknesses of the situation found will be discussed in relation to (1) the stated objectives of all the courses examined, and to the economic content of (2) arithmetic courses, (3) science courses, (4) social studies courses, (5) general courses.

OBJECTIVES OF ALL COURSES

The outstanding weakness of most of the courses examined is their failure to state any aims bearing on education for economic competence except conventional ones, such as the inculcation of thrift and respect for property.

In a small proportion of courses the need for economic education is amply recognized in the statement of philosophy and aims. Some of these courses list the detailed outcomes to be sought, and give abundant suggestions to teachers for achieving them; others merely indicate the aims in rather general terms and give no guidance as to methods or materials for attaining the aims.

Courses from the Southeast and the Southwest are stronger with respect to stating objectives bearing on economic competence than courses from other areas. The importance of raising the economic level of the people through education of the oncoming generation is clearly recognized by course of study writers in Alabama, Arkansas, Florida, Georgia, Mississippi, Missouri, Tennessee, Texas, and Virginia. The Virginia course of study is also notable for its definite and detailed list of abilities and understandings desired as outcomes in the area of education for economic competence.

THE ECONOMIC CONTENT OF ARITHMETIC COURSES

The great weakness of the arithmetic courses analyzed is their neglect of the informational function of arithmetic. A second weakness is the tendency to supply, for purposes of practice in computation, fictitious costs, rates, and prices, when it would be almost as easy and considerably more educative for the children to ascertain and use the costs, rates, and prices which prevail in their own community. A third weakness is the tendency to base problems on the activities pertaining to the higher income levels, as in computing a budget for a family with an income of three or four thousand dollars a year.

The strength of the situation lies in such courses as those of Illinois, Minneapolis, Oregon, Fort Worth (Texas), and Springfield (Massachusetts), which stress the arithmetic of daily life.

THE ECONOMIC CONTENT OF SCIENCE COURSES

Almost the only topics having a bearing on economic competence that occur frequently in science courses are those related to conservation. The application of science to the affairs of the farm and the household is treated in but a small proportion of the courses. Little attention is given in any course to the selection of goods and to community problems of health, housing, and diet.

A few science courses, including those of Maryland, Massachusetts, the State of New York, Amarillo (Texas), and Madison (Wisconsin), are notable for their consistency in relating scientific principles to the problems of the home and the farm.

THE ECONOMIC CONTENT OF SOCIAL STUDIES COURSES

In a sizable minority of the courses, geography and history are still kept separate. Where this is the case the content is likely to be organized in logical outlines rather than around persistent problems of living. While many topics having potential implications for economic competence are found in such outlines, these implications are not likely to be brought out. Industries, for example, are covered in all geography outlines for fifth and sixth grades, but with few exceptions the treatment is purely descriptive and ignores the opportunities for occupational guidance and consumer education, and for consideration of social-economic problems related to the industry in question. In fusion courses in the social studies these weaknesses are less conspicuous.

In social studies units dealing with a foreign country, too much emphasis is likely to be laid on the picturesque rather than on really important facts, such as the country's conservation and economic problems and the ways it is meeting them. The fact that some of the Netherlanders wear wooden shoes is of no more interest and of decidedly less consequence than their remarkable achievements in providing good housing for most of the population. The fact that certain towns in southern France derive the full support of their community services from the sale of nuts grown on the shade trees which line their streets deserves consideration quite as much as the costumes worn in the villages on festival days. The time has come for more courses like those of Fort Worth and Houston, Texas, in which other countries are shown to be occupied with the same social-economic problems as our own.

The great strength of the social studies in education for economic competence becomes apparent in elementary programs of which the social studies are the core, as those of Houston (Texas) and Binghamton (New York), and in courses emphasizing problems of home, community, state, region, as those of Kansas, and Madison, Wisconsin.

THE ECONOMIC CONTENT OF GENERAL COURSES

From the standpoint of education for economic competence, the outstanding weakness of general courses is their tendency to maintain strict divisions between the various blocks of subject matter. Where arithmetic,.art, English, science, and the social studies are kept separate, the emphasis is laid on learning the skills and informational content of each subject, and the applications to real life situations, which tend to transcend subject matter divisions, are not so likely to be developed.

The more nearly the general course becomes integrated, the more readily can it be organized about life problems, and the richer, therefore, its contribution to education for economic competence. The general courses of Hamilton County (Tennessee), Glencoe (Illinois), Mississippi, and Virginia demonstrate how a high degree of integration results in greatly increased attention to the skills and understandings necessary for economic competence. The trend toward integration is, therefore, the principal strength of the general courses.

ADDITIONAL PROBLEMS WHICH SHOULD BE INVESTIGATED

Investigation of such problems as the following would be of service to curriculum workers and to those responsible for the education of teachers:

1. What economic generalizations do the American people want taught to the oncoming generation?

2. What would the parents of elementary school children like these children to learn in school in any area of education for economic competence?

3. What answers do children give to direct questions as to the explanation for various economic conditions and relations? What answers do adults give? What answers do elementary teachers give?

4. What economic shortages exist in a given community or region that might be met through a suitable long-term program of education? What are the best procedures for discovering these shortages and working out a plan of community education to meet them?

5. What learnings in the area of economics can reasonably be expected from field trips and from community studies by children in the first six grades?

6. What is being taught about the problems of unemployment and relief in classes where many of the children come from families that may some time during the year require relief? In other classes?

7. What economic ideas are presented in elementary textbooks, and what do elementary teachers think of these ideas?

8. What outcomes do elementary teachers seek in any area of education for economic competence? What experiences do they provide in trying to attain these outcomes?

9. To what extent does the education and experience of elementary teachers prepare them to educate for economic competence? What do elementary teachers know in this area?

10. If elementary teachers are to educate for economic competence, what changes in teacher education and selection are indicated?

11. How can the outcomes of education for economic competence be measured?

RECOMMENDATIONS

The data gathered in this investigation lead to four recommendations for the writers of elementary courses of study.

I. That the attention of elementary teachers be directed to the importance of providing experiences which will contribute to the child's growth in economic competence.

II. That the desired outcomes of education for economic competence be formulated jointly by educators, parents, and child psychologists.

III. That in determining the outcomes to be sought, consideration be given to how the elementary school may contribute to the understandings necessary to achieve the democratic control of economic power and a wider distribution of the products of industry and agriculture.

IV. That ample problems and activities be suggested for the benefit of teachers who may wish guidance in developing the desired abilities and understandings.

With respect to the seven major groups of topics, which are likely to be the framework of any program of education for economic competence in the elementary school, the following recommendations are made:

I. *Industries and Occupations in the Modern World.* That so far as possible industries and occupations be studied at first hand. That proportionately less attention be given to the processes of production, and more attention be given, on appropriate grade levels, to the worth of the product and its selection and use by consumers, to occupational conditions, and to the characteristics of a machine civilization as illustrated by the given industry. That the dependence of each industry upon natural resources be emphasized. That the capacity of the construction industry to supply our need for good housing be considered in a simple fashion. That the recreation industry, and, in the sixth grade, the power industry and its dramatic potentialities, receive as much attention as other industries.

II. *Home Life in Our Community.* That this group of topics be considered in the intermediate grades as well as in the primary. That at least above the first grade, more real and fewer purely make-believe activities be suggested. That more emphasis be given to household science and arts. That more activities be designed to show ways in which low- and medium-income families may use their existing resources to better advantage in filling their most essential needs for food, clothing, shelter, and medical care. That the program be adapted to local needs and conditions, and the cooperation of parents be solicited. That a sustained effort be made to improve "home life in our community" through community-wide education.

III. *Conservation.* That on the intermediate level the economic importance of conservation be taught, and the conservation of soil, minerals, natural beauty, and human resources receive more attention. That the consequences of continued neglect of conservation be illustrated by reference to our own country, and particularly to the region in which the pupils live. That achievements in conservation, whether under public or private auspices, and the advantages of regional planning in the development of resources be presented. That ways in which pupils may participate in conservation be suggested.

IV. *Local Community Services.* That these be taken up in the intermediate grades as well as in the primary. That consideration be given to welfare agencies and their support. That well-managed community services be viewed as an addition to the income of the community. That the economies that may be expected from an expanded program of public health, housing, and social security be considered. That in the sixth grade some elementary information be gathered about the chief kinds of taxes and upon whom they fall.

V. *Characteristics of a Machine Civilization.* That this group of topics be presented on the fifth and sixth grade level in connection with industries and occupations, or, in historical units, in connection with the transition from a handicraft economy to an industrial economy. That the practical consequences of interdependence and mass production be discussed. That the possibilities of attaining an adequate standard of living for all the people of the United States be discussed. That insofar as problems like unemployment and poverty are dealt with—and they can hardly be kept out of the life-related curriculum—attention be focused on successful experiments in meeting them in the United States and in other industrial countries that are being studied.

VI. *Money Management.* That the tendency to ignore this group of topics be corrected. That children should be helped to appreciate the amount of money which parents have to spend and the many demands upon the family income. That children be helped to discover the possibilities for adding to the family's real income by self-service and the fuller use of community services. That children be helped to evaluate the comparative satisfactions that different expenditures may bring and to become conscious of the underlying values. That ways be suggested for children to participate in planning for and spending money for school and other educational or community purposes. That opportunities for evaluating advertisements be utilized. That giving to organizations for community welfare be taught as a responsibility and privilege of all citizens in a democracy save those in actual want. That when interest is taken up in the sixth grade some attention be given to the cost of the various forms of consumer credit.

VII. *Business Practices and Organization.* That in community study and the study of occupations and industries, attention be directed to the manner in which businesses are organized and controlled. That the differences between a cooperatively owned business and one that is privately owned be explored. That mention be made of outstanding instances of government ownership in the United States and in other countries being studied. That not merely the receiving of savings deposits but the various services of banks be considered.

SOME FURTHER IMPLICATIONS OF THIS STUDY

So far as courses of study give evidence of what is going on in the elementary schools of the United States, it is apparent that in many places not much attention is being given to developing an understanding of the economic aspects of life. The question inevitably arises, Why should this be so?

Two explanations may be advanced:

(1) The fear of antagonizing vested interests, such as advertisers and economically privileged groups, who may regard the teaching of certain facts and generalizations about the economic structure as subversive because opposed to their interests.

(2) Poor preparation in economics on the part of course of study writers and teachers. This could account for the failure to see opportunities for developing economic understandings, and for the belief that economic education should be deferred to the twelfth grade or later.

It seems probable that both fear of vested interests and poor preparation in economics are responsible for the paucity of economic objectives and materials in the majority of curriculum bulletins. That the importance of the former may have been overrated is suggested by the existence of a not inconsiderable number of bulletins which are rich in economic materials, and the existence of a few bulletins which suggest the teachings of generalizations that, if widely accepted, might lead to restrictions on economic privilege.

The curriculum bulletins which are outstanding for their economic content testify to a better-than-average preparation in economics on the part of their authors. To judge from the bulletins, this preparation includes an acquaintance with: (1) the principles and applications of personal economics, household economics, and the economics of welfare, and (2) the economic history of the United States, including the historical background of modern economic problems.

If all elementary teachers had a similar preparation, they would doubtless discover ways to use the everyday experiences and observations of children as a basis of education for economic competence. Fortified by knowledge of the facts, they would not be afraid to let children ask questions and discuss any of the economic problems of which they become aware. Furthermore, they would be able to set an example of economic competence which would be of value.

There seems little reason to suppose that teachers as a whole are more economically competent than other citizens. If they are not, they must themselves be educated in economics of a simple and functional sort before the schools can hope to accomplish much in preparing boys and girls to participate effectively in the varied economic activity of our time.

Bibliography

1. AMERICAN HISTORICAL ASSOCIATION. Commission on the Social Studies in the Schools. *Conclusions and Recommendations.* Charles Scribner's Sons, New York, 1934.
2. BONSER, FREDERICK AND MOSSMAN, LOIS. *Industrial Arts in the Elementary School.* The Macmillan Co. New York, 1935.
3. BRUNER, H. B. "Some Requirements of the Elementary School Curriculum." *Teachers College Record,* Vol. 39, pp. 273–286, January, 1938.
4. BRUNER, H. B. *What Our Schools Are Teaching.* Bureau of Publications, Teachers College, Columbia University, 1941.
4a. CAREY, ALICE E., HANNA, PAUL R., AND MERIAM, J. L. *Catalog: Units of Work, Activities, Projects, etc., to 1931.* Bureau of Publications, Teachers College, Columbia University, 1932.
5. CHASE, SARA E. "Individual Differences in the Experience of Children." (Unpublished.) Master's thesis, University of Chicago, 1927.
6. CLARK, HAROLD F. *Economic Theory and Correct Occupational Distribution.* Bureau of Publications, Teachers College, Columbia University, 1931.
7. COE, GEORGE A. *Law and Freedom in the Schools.* University of Chicago Press, 1924.
8. DALE, EDGAR. "Economics for Children." *Educational Research Bulletin,* Vol. X, No. 14, pp. 381–384, October 8, 1930.
9. EDUCATIONAL POLICIES COMMISSION. *Education and Economic Well-Being in American Democracy.* Washington, D. C., 1940.
10. EDUCATIONAL POLICIES COMMISSION. *The Purposes of Education in American Democracy.* Washington, D. C., 1938.
11. FARTHING, DOROTHY K. AND GORMAN, FRANK H. "The Selection of Modern Problems for Study in the Elementary School." *Educational Method,* Vol. XVIII, pp. 243–245, February, 1939.
12. GAVIAN, RUTH WOOD. "Children's Experiences with Money." *Social Education,* Vol. II, pp. 166–168, March, 1938.
13. GILLETTE, SISTER MARY DE PAUL. "Plan to Enrich the Curricula of a Group of Elementary and Secondary Parochial Schools to Meet the Interests and Needs of Pupils with Respect to Buying Goods." Ed. D. project report, Teachers College, Columbia University, 1936. (Manuscript.)

14. HARAP, HENRY. *The Education of the Consumer: A Study in Curriculum Material.* The Macmillan Co., New York, 1924.

15. HARAP, HENRY. *An Index to Units in Eighty-Nine Activity Curricula.* Curriculum Laboratory. George Peabody College, Nashville, Tenn., 1938. (Mimeo.)

16. HEFFERNAN, HELEN. "Redirection in Curriculum Making." In *Current Curricular Trends in Elementary Education.* Ninth Yearbook of California Elementary Principals' Association. 1937.

17. HOCKETT, JOHN A. "Facing Realities in Elementary School Social Studies." *California Journal of Elementary Education,* Vol. 4, pp. 136–147, February, 1936.

18. HOFFMAN, HELEN DUEY. "The Teacher as a Stimulating Force in the Community for Better Housing." *Childhood Education,* Vol. 14, pp. 26–29, September, 1937.

19. JUDD, CHARLES H. "Certain Neglected Social Institutions." *Elementary School Journal,* Vol. 25, pp. 254–263, December, 1924.

20. KELLEY, T. L. and KREY, A. C. *Tests and Measurements in the Social Sciences.* Charles Scribner's Sons, New York, 1934.

21. LEWIS, DORA S. "The Teaching of Buymanship." In *Proceedings* of the Seventy-Fourth Annual Meeting of the National Education Association. 1936.

22. LOGAN, S. R. "Economic Citizenship in the School Community." *Progressive Education,* Vol. 11, pp. 134–138, June, 1934.

22a. McCRACKEN, THOMAS C. AND LAMB, HELEN E. *Occupational Information in the Elementary Schools.* Houghton Mifflin Co., Boston, 1923.

23. MITCHELL, F. C. "Ability of Fifth Grade Pupils to Understand Certain Social Concepts." *California Journal of Elementary Education,* Vol. 4, pp. 20–28, August, 1935.

24. MORGAN, J. E. "Teaching Economics to Children." *Journal of National Education Association,* Vol. 27, pp. 33–34, February, 1938.

25. NATIONAL RESOURCES COMMITTEE. *Consumer Incomes in the United States: Their Distribution in 1935–36.* Government Printing Office, Washington, D. C., 1938.

26. NEWLON, JESSE H. *Education for Democracy in Our Time.* McGraw-Hill Co., New York, 1939.

27. NEWLON, JESSE H. "Freedom of Teaching." Chap. X. (See No. 28)

28. NEWLON, JESSE H. "The Teaching Profession as a Functional Group in Society." Chap. XI. In *The Teacher and Society.* First Yearbook of the John Dewey Society (William H. Kilpatrick, edr.). D. Appleton-Century Co., New York, 1937.

29. NEW YORK STATE ASSOCIATION OF ELEMENTARY PRINCIPALS. Edu-

cation Progress Committee. *A Study of Children's Interests in Social and Economic Questions.* Preliminary report, 1940. (Typescript.)

30. O'NEIL, FLORENCE C. AND McCORMICK, MARY G. *Everyday Behavior of Elementary School Children: Report of a Study of the Twenty-Four-Hour Day Health Behavior of 3512 Individual Children.* University of the State of New York Bulletin No. 1057. Albany, 1934.

31. PAYNE, RESEDA BERRY. *Investigation into the Buying Experiences of Fifth and Sixth Grade Girls at Jackson School.* Master's thesis, University of Cincinnati, 1932. (Unpublished.)

32. REEVES, GRACE G. "Home Living Problems." *Journal of Home Economics,* Vol. XXX, pp. 289–292, May, 1938.

33. SHERMAN, HARRY. *The Promises Men Live By: A New Approach to Economics.* Random House, New York, 1938.

34. STODDARD, ALEXANDER J. "Providing an Adequate Economic Education." *Nation's Schools,* Vol. 16, pp. 27–28, September, 1935.

35. WARREN, DOROTHY AND BURTON, W. H. "Knowledge of Simple Business Practices Possessed by Intermediate Grade Pupils." *Elementary School Journal,* Vol. 35, pp. 511–516, March, 1935.

36. WELLING, JANE BETSY AND CALKINS, CHARLOTTE W. *Social and Industrial Studies for the Elementary Grades: Based on Needs for Food, Clothing, Shelter, Implements, and Records.* J. B. Lippincott Co., Philadelphia, 1923.

GENERAL BULLETINS TABULATED

37. ALABAMA. *Course of Study for Elementary Schools.* State Department of Education, Montgomery, Ala., 1930.

38. AMARILLO, TEXAS, *A Tentative Course of Study for Grades One to Three.* Board of Education, Amarillo, Tex., 1937. (Mimeo.)

39. ARKANSAS. *A Tentative Course of Study for Arkansas Schools: Elementary Section.* State Department of Education, Little Rock, Ark., 1936.

40. BOSTON, MASSACHUSETTS. *Course of Study for the Elementary Schools. First Grade,* 1936. *Third Grade,* 1936. *Fourth Grade,* 1926. *Fifth Grade,* 1926. *Sixth Grade,* 1926. School Committee, Boston, Mass.

41. COLORADO. *Course of Study for Elementary Schools.* State Department of Education, Denver, Colo., 1936.

42. FLORIDA. *Course of Study for Florida Elementary Schools.* State Department of Public Instruction, Tallahassee, Fla., 1933.

43. GEORGIA. *Course of Study for Elementary Schools.* State Department of Education, Atlanta, Ga., 1932.

44. GLENCOE, ILLINOIS. *Experimental Curriculum Outline for Glencoe Public Schools.* Board of Education, Glencoe, Ill., 1937. (Mimeo.)

45. HAMILTON COUNTY, TENNESSEE. *Professional Yearbook. Elementary Schools. 1936–37, Grades 5–6. 1937–38, Grades 1–2. 1938–39, Grades 3–4. 1939–40, Grade 3.* Hamilton County Board of Education, Tenn. (Mimeo.)

46. IDAHO. *Course of Study for Elementary Schools of Idaho.* State Department of Public Instruction, Boise, Idaho, 1931.

47. IOWA. *Course of Study for Elementary Schools.* State Department of Public Instruction, Des Moines, Iowa, 1928.

48. KANSAS. *Course of Study for the Elementary Schools of Kansas.* State Department of Public Instruction, Topeka, Kan., 1932.

49. KENTUCKY. *Teachers' Manual and Courses of Study for the Elementary Schools.* State Board of Education, Frankfort, Ky., 1931.

50. KERN COUNTY, CALIFORNIA. *Manual for Elementary Grades: Intermediate Unit.* Board of Education, Kern County, Calif., 1932–33.

51. LOS ANGELES. *Their First Years in School, A Course of Study for Kindergarten and the First Two Years of the Elementary Schools of Los Angeles County.* County Board of Education, Los Angeles, Calif., 1939.

52. LOS ANGELES. *Teachers' Guide: Intermediate Unit.* County Board of Education, Los Angeles, Calif., 1931.

53. MAINE. *Elementary School Curriculum.* State Department of Education, Augusta, Me., 1931.

54. MICHIGAN. *Instructional Guide for Elementary Schools.* Department of Public Instruction, Lansing, Mich., 1936.

55. MINNESOTA. *Curriculum for Elementary Schools.* State Department of Education, St. Paul, Minn., 1928.

56. MISSISSIPPI. *A Guide for Curriculum Reorganization in the Elementary School.* State Board of Education, Jackson, Miss., 1937.

57. MISSOURI. *Missouri at Work on the Public School Curriculum; Course of Study for Elementary Grades.* State Department of Education, Jefferson City, Mo., 1937.

58. MONTANA. *A Course of Study for Rural and Graded Elementary Schools.* State Department of Public Instruction, Helena, Mont., 1931.

59. MUNCIE, INDIANA. *Unified Primary Activities: Course of Study for Grades 1, 2, and 3.* Board of Education, Muncie, Ind., 1938. (Mimeo.)

60. NEVADA. *Course of Study for the Elementary Grades. Part I* and *Part II.* 2 Vol. Department of Public Instruction, Carson City, Nev., 1937.

61. NEW HAMPSHIRE. *Program of Studies Recommended for the Elementary Schools of New Hampshire.* State Board of Education, Concord, N. H., 1930.

62. NEW MEXICO. *Course of Study for Elementary Schools.* State Department of Education, Santa Fe, N. M., 1930.

63. NORTH CAROLINA. *A Study of Curriculum Problems of the North Carolina Public Schools.* State Department of Public Instruction, Raleigh, N. C., 1935.

64. NORTH DAKOTA. *Elementary Courses of Study, with Suggested Daily Program and Organization for Rural Schools.* Department of Public Instruction, Bismarck, N. D., 1934.

65. PENNSYLVANIA. *Manual and Courses of Study for Elementary Schools.* State Department of Public Instruction, Harrisburg, Pa., 1925.

66. SANDUSKY, OHIO. *Course of Study: Elementary Grades.* Board of Education, Sandusky, Ohio, 1934. (Mimeo.)

67. SOUTH DAKOTA. *Elementary Course of Study for the Public Schools of South Dakota.* State Department of Education, Pierre, S. D., 1933.

68. TEXAS. *Course of Study. Years One through Three.* (See 69.)

69. TEXAS. *Course of Study. Years Four through Six. 2 Vol.* State Department of Education, Austin, Tex., 1938.

70. TULSA, OKLAHOMA. *A Course of Study for Kindergarten and Grades One, Two, Three.* Board of Education, Tulsa, Okla., 1938. (Mimeo.)

71. UTAH. *Course of Study for Elementary Schools.* State Department of Public Instruction, Salt Lake City, Utah, 1928.

72. VERMILION COUNTY, ILLINOIS. *Course of Study for the Elementary Schools of Vermilion County.* County Board of Education, Danville, Ill., 1937.

73. VIRGINIA. *Tentative Course of Study for Virginia Elementary Schools, Grades I–VII.* State Board of Education, Richmond, Va., 1937.

74. WASHINGTON. *Elementary Course of Study.* State Department of Education, Olympia, Wash., 1930.

75. WEST VIRGINIA. *Program of Study for Elementary Schools.* State Department of Education, Charleston, W. Va., 1937.

76. WISCONSIN. *Courses of Study for the State Graded Schools and Grades below High School.* State Department of Education, Madison, Wis., 1929.

ARITHMETIC BULLETINS TABULATED

77. ABERDEEN, SOUTH DAKOTA. *Course of Study in Arithmetic for Elementary Grades.* Board of Education, Aberdeen, S. D., 1935–36.

78. AMARILLO, TEXAS. *Arithmetic: A Tentative Course of Study for Grades Four, Five, Six.* Board of Education, Amarillo, Tex., 1938. (Mimeo.)

79. ARIZONA. *Course of Study for Elementary Schools: Arithmetic.* State Department of Education, Phoenix, Ariz., 1933.

80. BALTIMORE, MARYLAND. *Arithmetic Course of Study for Grades Four, Five, and Six.* Department of Education, Baltimore, Md., 1929 Revision.

   Supplement to the Arithmetic Course of Study for Grades Four, Five, and Six. Department of Education, Baltimore, Md., 1931.

81. CHARLESTON, SOUTH CAROLINA. *Elementary Course of Study: Arithmetic.* Board of Education, Charleston, S. C., 1930.

82. CHEYENNE, WYOMING. *Arithmetic Course of Study, Grades One to Six.* Board of Education, Cheyenne, Wyo., 1936.

83. CHICAGO, ILLINOIS. *Course of Study in Arithmetic. Grade 4. Grade 5. Grade 6.* 3 Vol. Board of Education, Chicago, Ill., 1939. (Mimeo.)

84. CLEVELAND, OHIO. *Arithmetic: A Tentative List of Objectives for the Upper Elementary Division.* Board of Education, Cleveland, Ohio., 1938. (Mimeo.)

85. DENVER, COLORADO. *Arithmetic, Grades Three, Four, Five, and Six.* Board of Education, Denver, Colo., 1933. (Mimeo.)

86. DETROIT. *Tentative Course of Study in Elementary School Arithmetic.* Board of Education, Detroit, Mich., 1930.

87. EVANSTON, ILLINOIS. *Arithmetic Syllabus for Intermediate Grades.* Board of Education, Evanston, Ill., 1934. (Mimeo.)

88. FORT WORTH, TEXAS. *Mathematics: A Tentative Course of Study for Grades Four, Five, and Six.* Board of Education, Fort Worth, Tex., 1936. (Mimeo.)

89. GREENSBORO, NORTH CAROLINA. *Tentative Course of Study in Arithmetic, Grades 1–6.* Board of Education, Greensboro, N. C., 1932–33.

90. IDAHO. *Curriculum Thinking, A Study Guide Prepared by the Idaho State Arithmetic Committee.* State Department of Education, Boise, Idaho, 1938. (Mimeo.)

91. ILLINOIS. *Mathematics Area of the Rural School Curriculum Guide (Tentative).* Department of Public Instruction, Springfield, Ill., no date. (Mimeo.)

92. INDIANAPOLIS, INDIANA. *Course of Study in Mathematics for the Elementary Schools, Grades 1–6.* Board of School Commissioners, Indianapolis, Ind., 1936.

93. KANSAS CITY, MISSOURI. *Tentative Revision of Course of Study in Arithmetic, Intermediate and Upper Grades.* Board of Education, Kansas City, Mo., 1938. (Mimeo.)

94. LONG BEACH, CALIFORNIA. *Arithmetic Guide for Teachers of Primary and Intermediate Grades.* Board of Education, Long Beach, Calif., 1938. (Mimeo.)

95. LOUISIANA. *Course of Study in Arithmetic for Grades Four, Five, Six and Seven.* State Department of Education, Baton Rouge, La., 1930.

96. MINNEAPOLIS, MINNESOTA. *Course of Study in Arithmetic for Elementary School.* Board of Education, Minneapolis, Minn., 1935.

97. MISSOURI. *Teaching Arithmetic.* State Department of Education, Jefferson City, Mo., 1930.

98. MUNCIE, INDIANA. *Tentative Course of Study in Elementary Mathematics, Grades 1–6.* Board of Education, Muncie, Ind., 1933.

99. MUSKOGEE, OKLAHOMA. *Course of Study in Arithmetic for Elementary Schools, Grades 1–6.* Board of Education, Muskogee, Okla., 1930.

100. NEW JERSEY. *A Teachers' Guide Book and Course of Study in Arithmetic, for Grades One to Eight.* State Department of Public Instruction, Trenton, N. J., 1930.

101. NEW YORK. *Syllabus for Elementary Schools. Arithmetic.* University of the State of New York, Albany, N. Y., 1924.

102. OKLAHOMA CITY, OKLAHOMA. *Revised Course of Study: Arithmetic: Grades I–VI.* Board of Education, Oklahoma City, Okla., 1936–37. (Mimeo.)

103. OREGON. *Course of Study, Arithmetic.* State Department of Education, Salem, Ore., 1929.

104. PENNSYLVANIA. *Quantitative Aspects of Experiencing in the Elementary School.* State Department of Public Instruction, Harrisburg, Pa., 1939.

105. PERTH AMBOY, NEW JERSEY. *Tentative Course of Study, Mathematics, Part I, Grades 4–5–6.* Board of Education, Perth Amboy, N. J., 1938.

106. SACRAMENTO, CALIFORNIA. *Arithmetic, Grades 3–4–5–6.* Board of Education, Sacramento, Calif., 1931.

107. SAN ANTONIO, TEXAS. *Course of Study Monograph No. 3: Arithmetic.* Board of Education, San Antonio, Tex., 1936.

108. SAN MATEO COUNTY, CALIFORNIA. *Arithmetic Experiences: Primary and Intermediate Grades.* Board of Education, San Mateo County, Calif., 1939.

109. SOUTH DAKOTA. *Arithmetic Course of Study for Elementary Grades.* State Department of Public Instruction, Pierre, S. D., 1931.

110. SPRINGFIELD, MASSACHUSETTS. *Social Arithmetic in the Elementary Curriculum, Grades 3–6.* Board of Education, Springfield, Mass., 1938. (Mimeo.)

111. UTAH. *Course of Study in Arithmetic, Grades One to Eight.* State Department of Public Instruction, Salt Lake City, Utah, 1936.

112. VERMONT. *Courses of Study for Elementary and Rural Schools: Part III. Arithmetic.* State Board of Education, Montpelier, Vt., 1928.

113. WATERTOWN, NEW YORK. *Tentative Revision of Arithmetic Syllabus,*

Elementary Schools. Board of Education, Watertown, N. Y., 1936. (Mimeo.)

114. WYOMING. *Course of Study for Elementary Schools: Arithmetic.* State Department of Education, Cheyenne, Wyo., 1937.

SOCIAL STUDIES BULLETINS TABULATED

115. ABERDEEN, SOUTH DAKOTA. *Course of Study in Social Studies: Primary Grades.* Board of Education, Aberdeen, S. D., 1935–36. (Mimeo.)

116. ABERDEEN, SOUTH DAKOTA. *Course of Study in Geography. Fourth Grade. Sixth Grade.* (With Supplementary Historical Units) 2 Vol. Board of Education, Aberdeen, S. D., 1935.

117. ARIZONA. *Course of Study for Elementary Schools of Arizona; Social Studies.* State Department of Education, Phoenix, Ariz., 1934.

118. ATLANTA, GEORGIA. *General Content of the Course of Study in the Social Sciences for the Elementary Schools.* Board of Education, Atlanta, Ga., 1934.

119. BERKELEY, CALIFORNIA. *Social Studies. Courses of Study for Grades 3 and 4. Courses of Study for Grades 5 and 6.* 2 Vol. Board of Education, Berkeley, Calif., 1932.

120. BINGHAMTON, NEW YORK. Units: *Life in the Middle Ages* (Grade 5B). *Life and Work in Our Great West* (Grade 5A). *How Agriculture Supplies Our Needs and Wants* (Grade 6B). *How Manufacturing Supplies Our Needs and Wants* (Grade 6A). 4 Vol. Board of Education, Binghamton, N. Y., 1938. (Mimeo.)

121. BROCKTON, MASSACHUSETTS. *Social Studies. Grade 1. Grade 2. Grade 3.* 3 Vol. Board of Education, Brockton, Mass., 1938. (Mimeo.)

122. CALIFORNIA. *Suggested Course of Study in the Social Studies for Elementary Schools, Revised.* State Department of Education, Sacramento, Calif., 1933.

123. CHEYENNE, WYOMING. *Social Science Course of Study: Grade Six.* Board of Education, Cheyenne, Wyo., 1939. (Mimeo.)

124. CLEVELAND HEIGHTS, OHIO. *Elementary School Course of Study: Social Studies in Grades IV–VI.* Board of Education, Cleveland Heights, Ohio, 1930. (Mimeo.) Grade VI only tabulated.

125. CONNECTICUT. *Social Studies in the Primary Grades.* State Board of Education, Hartford, Conn., 1932.

126. DELAWARE. *Integrated Curriculum Units: Social Studies. Grade 1. Grade 2. Grade 3. Grade 4.* 4 Vol. State Department of Public Instruction, Dover, Del., 1938. (Mimeo.)

127. DENVER, COLORADO. *Kindergarten-Primary Course of Study: Social Studies.* Board of Education, Denver, Colo., 1932.

128. Denver, Colorado. *Social Science: Grades Three, Four, Five, and Six.* Board of Education, Denver, Colo., 1931.
129. Des Moines, Iowa. *Social Studies Course of Study, Kindergarten to Grade II.* Board of Education, Des Moines, Iowa, 1934. (Mimeo.)
130. Des Moines, Iowa. *Social Studies,* Grades V and VI. Board of Education, Des Moines, Iowa, 1936. (Mimeo.)
131. Detroit. *Course of Study in Elementary Social Science.* Board of Education, Detroit, Mich., 1932. (Mimeo.)
132. Fort Worth, Texas. *A Tentative Course of Study in Social Studies. Grade One. Grade Two. Grade Three. Grade Four. Grade Five.* Grade Six. 6 Vol. 1933. (Mimeo.)
133. Fort Worth, Texas. *Supplementary Units, Social Studies. Grade One. Grade Two. Grade Three. Grade Four. Grade Five. Grade Six.* 6 Vol. Board of Education, Fort Worth, Texas, 1938. (Mimeo.)
134. Grand Rapids, Michigan. *Tentative Course of Study in Social Studies for Kindergarten-First Grade.* Board of Education, Grand Rapids, Mich., 1935. (Mimeo.) Grade One only was tabulated.
135. Hartford, Connecticut. *A Course in Social Studies for the Public Schools through Grade Six.* State Board of Education, Hartford, Conn., 1929.

Houston, Texas. Integrated Curriculum Units:
136. *City and Country Life* (Low Second), 1930–31.
137. *Primitive Life* (High Second), 1931–32.
138. *Food, Clothing, and Shelter* (Unit 1, Third).
139. *Transportation and Communication* (Unit 2, Third).
140. *Life in Cold Lands* (Unit 3, Third).
141. *Life in Hot Lands* (Unit 4, Third), 1931–32.
142. *Life in Ancient Egypt and Mesopotamia* (Unit 1, Fourth).
143. *A Study of Life in Ancient Phoenicia and Palestine* (Unit 2, Fourth).
144. *Life in Ancient Greece and Rome* (Unit 3, Fourth).
145. *Living in a Temperate Lowland* (Unit 4, Fourth).
146. *Living in a Mountainous Region* (Unit 5, Fourth).
147. *Living in an Insular Region: Japanese Empire* (Unit 6, Fourth), 1930–31.
148. *From the Old World to the New* (Unit 1, Fifth).
149. *Making of Americans* (Unit 2, Fifth).
150. *Life on the American Frontier* (Unit 3, Fifth).
151. *From Cotton Field to Factory* (Unit 4, Fifth).
152. *Transportation* (Unit 1, Low Sixth).
153. *How Communication Increases Interdependence* (Unit 2, Low Sixth).
154. *Earth and Its People* (Unit 3, Low Sixth).
155. *How Our Modern Civilization Depends upon Exchange* (Unit 1, High Sixth), 1931–32.

156. *How Our Community Depends upon the Co-operation of Its Citizens* (Unit 3, High Sixth), 1932–33. Board of Education, Houston, Tex. (Mimeo.)

157. IOWA. *Guide for Teaching Geography in the Elementary Grades.* State Department of Public Instruction, Des Moines, Iowa, 1935.

158. IOWA. *Guide for Teaching History in the Elementary Grades.* 1935–36.

159. IDAHO. *Social Studies and Science Grades 1–8.* State Department of Education, Boise, Idaho, 1939. (Mimeo.) (Courses for Grades One, Two, and Three only were tabulated.)

160. INDIANA. *Tentative Course of Study in Elementary Social Studies.* Department of Public Instruction, Indianapolis, Ind., 1931.

161. ITHACA, NEW YORK. *Course of Study in Social Studies for Grades 3–6.* Board of Education, Ithaca, N. Y., 1936. (Mimeo.)

162. JOLIET, ILLINOIS. *Tentative Course in Social Studies, Grades One to Three.* Board of Education, Joliet, Ill., 1937. (Mimeo.)

163. KANSAS. *Unit Program in Social Studies.* State Department of Education, Topeka, Kan., 1936.

164. KANSAS CITY, MISSOURI. *Social Studies for Primary Grades.* Board of Education, Kansas City, Mo., 1930. (Mimeo.)

165. LAKEWOOD, OHIO. *Social Sciences. A Tentative Course of Study for First Grade. A Tentative Course of Study for Second Grade. A Tentative Course of Study for Third Grade.* 3 Vol. Board of Education, Lakewood, Ohio, 1931. (Mimeo.)

166. LAKEWOOD, OHIO. *A Tentative Course of Study in Geography: Fourth Grade. A Tentative Course of Study in Geography: Fifth Grade.* 2 Vol. Board of Education, Lakewood, Ohio, 1931.

167. MADISON, WISCONSIN. *Social Studies. Grade One. Grade Two. Grade Three. Grade Four. Grade Five. Grade Six.* 6 Vol. Board of Education, Madison, Wis., 1934. (Mimeo.)

168. MARYLAND. *Goals in Social Studies for Primary Grades.* State Department of Education, Baltimore, Md., 1931.

169. MARYLAND. *Curriculum Materials in the Social Studies for Intermediate Grades.* State Department of Education, Baltimore, Md., 1938.

170. MISHAWAKA, INDIANA. *Social Science for Grades I, II, and III.* Board of Education, Mishawaka, Ind., 1935. (Mimeo.)

171. MONTCLAIR, NEW JERSEY. *Tentative Course of Study in the Social Studies in the Kindergarten, First, Second, and Third Grades.* Board of Education, Montclair, N. J., 1930. (Mimeo.)

172. MUNCIE, INDIANA. *Tentative Course of Study in Elementary Social Science, Grades 4 to 6.* Board of Education, Muncie, Ind., 1935.

173. NEW YORK. *Handbook for Rural Elementary Schools; the Social Studies Group.* University of the State of New York, Albany, N. Y., 1936.

174. OKLAHOMA CITY, OKLAHOMA. *Revised Course of Study: Social Science, Grades IV-VI*. Board of Education, Oklahoma City, Okla., 1936. (Mimeo.)

175. OMAHA, NEBRASKA. *Social Studies for Grades 4-6*. Board of Education, Omaha, Neb., 1936. (Mimeo.)

176. PENNSYLVANIA. *Course of Study in Social Studies. Grades One and Two. Grades Three and Four. Grades Five and Six*. 3 Vol. 1932. State Department of Public Instruction, Harrisburg, Pa.

177. PENNSYLVANIA. *Geographic Education in Elementary and Junior High Schools*. State Department of Public Instruction, Harrisburg, Pa., 1935.

178. PRINCETON, ILLINOIS. *Tentative Social Studies Curriculum, Grades 1-5*. Board of Education, Princeton, Ill., 1936. (Mimeo.)

179. PROVIDENCE, RHODE ISLAND. *Elementary School Social Science Curriculum. Grades 1B-1A; Grades 2B-2A; Grades 3B-3A*. 3 Vol. Department of Public Schools, Providence, R. I., 1936. (Mimeo.)

180. PROVIDENCE, RHODE ISLAND. *Geography Curriculum for Elementary Schools. Grade 4. Grade 5. Grade 6*. 3 Vol. Department of Public Schools, Providence, R. I., 1935. (Mimeo.)

181. PROVIDENCE, RHODE ISLAND. *History Curriculum for Elementary Schools. Grade 4. Grade 5. Grade 6*. 3 Vol. Department of Public Schools, Providence, R. I., 1935. (Mimeo.)

182. SAGINAW, MICHIGAN. *Suggested Integrated Curriculum Units Emphasizing Social Studies. Kindergarten, Grade One and Grade Two. Grades 3 and 4. Grades 5 and 6*. 3 Vol. Board of Education, Saginaw, Mich., 1939. (Mimeo.) (Grade 3 was not tabulated.)

183. ST. LOUIS, COUNTY OF. *The Teaching of the Social Studies*. County Board of Education, Clayton, Missouri, 1938. (Mimeo.) (Grades One, Two, and Three only were tabulated.)

184. ST. PAUL, MINNESOTA. *Tentative Course of Study in Social Studies and Related Subjects. Grade 1. Grade 2. Grade 3. Grade 4A. Grade 4B. Grade 5A. Grade 5B. Grade 6A. Grade 6B*. 9 Vol. Board of Education, St. Paul, Minn., 1935-36.

185. SAN MATEO COUNTY, CALIFORNIA. *The Social Studies for Rural Schools. Grades 1-8*. County Board of Education, Redwood City, Calif., 1932. (Mimeo.)

186. SOUTH CAROLINA. *Social Studies*. Elementary School Manual Series, Bulletin I. State Department of Education, Columbia, S. C., 1936. (Grades One, Two, and Three only were tabulated.)

187. SOUTH DAKOTA. *Social Studies Course of Study for Primary Grades*. State Department of Public Instruction, Pierre, S. D., 1931.

188. SOUTH DAKOTA. *Social Studies Including History, Civics, Geography, Science, and Hygiene for Intermediate Grades*. 1932.

189. SPRINGFIELD, MASSACHUSETTS. *Social Studies: A Tentative Course of Study for Kindergarten, and Grades 1, 2, and 3.* Board of Education, Springfield, Mass., 1931. (Mimeo.)

190. SPRINGFIELD, MASSACHUSETTS. *Social Studies: A Tentative Course of Study for Grades IV, V, VI.* Board of Education, Springfield, Mass., 1928. (Mimeo.)

191. UTAH. *A Unified Course in the Social Studies for the Elementary Schools of Utah.* State Department of Public Instruction, Salt Lake City, Utah, 1934. (Mimeo.)

192. VANCOUVER, WASHINGTON. *Social Studies Curriculum Handbook.* Board of Education, Vancouver, Wash., 1938. (Mimeo.)

193. WASHINGTON. *An Integrated Social Science Curriculum for Elementary Grades.* State Department of Public Instruction, Olympia, Wash., 1936. (Mimeo.)

SCIENCE BULLETINS TABULATED

194. AMARILLO, TEXAS. *Elementary Science: A Tentative Course of Study for Grades Four, Five, and Six.* Board of Education, Amarillo, Tex., 1938. (Mimeo.)

195. APPLETON, WISCONSIN. *Conservation: a Course of Study for Public Elementary Schools.* Board of Education, Appleton, Wis., 1937. (Mimeo.) Equivalent to a course in elementary science.

196. ARIZONA. *Course of Study for Elementary Schools of Arizona: Nature Study.* State Department of Education, Phoenix, Ariz., 1936. (Primary grades only tabulated.)

197. CALIFORNIA. *Suggested Course of Study in Science for Elementary Schools.* State Department of Education, Sacramento, Calif., 1932.

198. CHICAGO, ILLINOIS. *A Course of Study in Science and Nature Study for Fourth, Fifth, and Sixth Grades.* Board of Education, Chicago, Ill., 1932.

199. CONNECTICUT. *A Course of Study in Nature Study.* State Board of Education, Hartford, Conn., 1932.

200. DES MOINES, IOWA. *Course of Study in General Science, Grades III through VI.* Board of Education, Des Moines, Iowa, 1933. (Mimeo.)

201. FORT WORTH, TEXAS. *Science for the Elementary School: A Tentative Course of Study. Grade One. Grade Two. Grade Three.* 3 vol. Board of Education, Fort Worth, Tex., 1934. (Mimeo.)

202. GALLION, OHIO. *Course of Study for Elementary Science: Grades 1–6.* Board of Education, Gallion, Ohio, 1933–34. (Mimeo.)

203. HOUSTON, TEXAS. *Science for the Elementary School: A Tentative Course of Study. Grade One. Grade Two. Grade Three.* 3 Vol. Board of Education, Houston, Tex., 1934. (Mimeo.)

204. ILLINOIS. *Natural Science Area of the Rural School Curriculum Guide.* State Department of Public Instruction, Springfield, Ill., 1939. (Mimeo.)

205. INDIANA. *Tentative Course of Study in Elementary Science and Health.* State Department of Public Instruction, Indianapolis, Ind., 1931.

206. IOWA. *A Guide for Teaching Science in Grades One to Eight.* State Department of Public Instruction, Des Moines, Iowa, 1937.

207. JOLIET, ILLINOIS. *Tentative Course in Elementary Science.* 1931. (Mimeo.) (Grade One only was tabulated.)

208. KANSAS CITY, MISSOURI. *Tentative Course of Study in Nature Study and Elementary Science.* Board of Education, Kansas City, Mo., 1930.

209. MADISON, WISCONSIN. *Natural Science. Grade IV. Grade V. Grade VI.* 3 Vol. Board of Education, Madison, Wis., 1937. (Mimeo.)

210. MARYLAND. *Science in the Elementary School: Suggested Units for Grades 1–7.* State Department of Education, Baltimore, Md., 1933.

211. MASSACHUSETTS. *A Course of Study in Science for Elementary Schools.* State Department of Education, Boston, Mass., 1931.

212. MISHAWAKA, INDIANA. *Course of Study in Elementary Science for Grades One to Three.* 1939. (Mimeo.) (Grades One and Two only were tabulated.)

213. MONTGOMERY COUNTY, MARYLAND. *Science Course of Study: Grades 1–6.* Montgomery County Board of Education, Rockville, Maryland, 1934. (Mimeo.)

214. NEW YORK (CITY). *Course of Study in Nature Study for Elementary Schools.* Board of Education, New York, N. Y., 1927.

215. NEW YORK. *Elementary School Science.* University of the State of New York, Albany, N. Y., 1939.

216. OAKLAND, CALIFORNIA. *Tentative Outline of a Handbook in Science for Elementary Grades 4–6.* Board of Education, Okland, Calif., 1932.

217. OMAHA, NEBRASKA. *Science for the Elementary Grades.* Board of Education, Omaha, Neb., 1936. (Mimeo.)

218. OREGON. *Nature Study, Elementary Schools.* State Board of Education, Salem, Ore., 1937.

219. PITTSBURG, KANSAS. *Nature Study, Grades 2–6.* 1930–31. (Mimeo.)

220. SALT LAKE CITY, UTAH. *Course of Study in Natural Science.* Board of Education, Salt Lake City, Utah, 1929.

221. SAN MATEO COUNTY, CALIFORNIA. *Elementary Science, Grades 1–6, Rural Schools of San Mateo County.* San Mateo County Board of Education, Redwood City, Calif., 1934. (Mimeo.)

222. SOUTH CAROLINA. *Science.* Elementary School Manual Series, Bulletin III. State Department of Education, Columbia, S. C., 1936.

COURSES CITED BUT NOT TABULATED

223. ALABAMA. *Report of Committee on Point of View, Aims, and Scope.* State Department of Education, Montgomery, Ala., 1937.

224. ALLENTOWN, PENNSYLVANIA. *Community Services and the Community Chest.* Board of Education, Allentown, Pa., 1938. (Mimeo.)

225. ATLANTA, GEORGIA. *Living and Growing in the Home-School-Community: Kindergarten and Grades 1, 2, 3.* 1937.

226. ————. *Living and Growing in the Home-School-Community, Grades 4, 5, 6.* Board of Education, Atlanta, Ga., 1938. (Mimeo.)

227. BROCKTON, MASSACHUSETTS. *Geography and History for Social Living: Living in Our Country from Early Times to Now: Grade 5.* Board of Education, Brockton, Mass., 1938. (Mimeo.)

228. BRONXVILLE, NEW YORK. *Report of the Social Studies Committee of the Elementary Grades.* Board of Education, Bronxville, N. Y., 1939. (Mimeo.)

229. GEORGIA. *Guide to Curriculum Improvement.* State Department of Education, Atlanta, Ga., 1937.

230. HOUSTON, TEXAS. *Science Units for High Sixth Grade.* Board of Education, Houston, Tex., 1932. (Mimeo.)

231. LOUISIANA. *Louisiana Program for the Improvement of Instruction: Second Bulletin.* State Department of Education, Baton Rouge, La., 1936.

232. LOUISIANA. *Louisiana Program of Curriculum Development: Study Program.* State Department of Education, Baton Rouge, La., 1936.

233. MANHASSET, NEW YORK. *Tentative Social Studies Outline.* Board of Education, Manhasset, N. Y., 1939. (Mimeo.)

234. MICHIGAN. *Instructional Practices in Elementary Schools.* State Department of Public Instruction, Lansing, Mich., 1938.

235. MINNESOTA. *A Suggested Unit on Co-operation for Upper Grades.* State Department of Education, St. Paul, Minn., 1938. (Mimeo.)

236. OSSINING, NEW YORK. Grade IV, Unit IV: *Our Community and Westchester County.* Grade IV, Unit VII: *New York's Part in Supplying the Needs of the World.* Grade VI, Unit VI: *How the Miners of Coal and Iron Have Helped in the Development of Our Country.* Board of Education, Ossining, N. Y., 1938. (Mimeo.)

237. TENNESSEE. *Looking Ahead with Tennessee Schools.* State Department of Education, Nashville, Tenn., 1937.

238. TEXAS. *Tentative Course of Study: Grades One to Six.* State Department of Education, Austin, Tex., 1936.

Index